What business leaders are saying about
The No-Panic Plan for Presenters

"Whether you make presentations three times a week, three times a month, or three times a year, you will find *The No-Panic Plan for Presenters* to be practical and personal. Practical because it is filled with useful checklists and the reasons behind every item on the list. Personal because Mandi, a certified speaking professional with an impressive client list, shares her own experiences. *The No-Panic Plan for Presenters* is so useful that my copy can always be found in my briefcase as I'm on the way to my next presentation."

Phil Hardwick
Stennis Institute of Government
Author of The Great American Mystery Series

■ ■ ■

"Keep this book within arm's reach at all times. It is your blueprint for a successful presentation. Whether you are delivering a message to the PTA, for the board of directors, or speaking on the main stage, these ideas will help you have more impact and influence with the people you serve best."

Mark LeBlanc
Professional Speaker, Small Business Success
Author of Growing Your Business *and* Never Be the Same

■ ■ ■

"Thank you so much for your contribution to our annual client event. Most of our guests are executives of corporations and found many aspects of it pertinent to their daily business lives. I cannot tell you the number of times your name has been mentioned as we have prepared for various formal and informal speaking events. Not to mention, we would not dare travel to a speaking engagement without *The No-Panic Plan for Presenters* close at hand!"

Gloria Grand
Vice President of Marketing
U.S. Bank

How presenters are practically using the tips and techniques in *The No-Panic Plan for Presenters*

"I delivered my outgoing speech last night to the chapter. The event was fabulous with 100 people. I used everything you taught me! I can't tell you how much you helped me. I had the room engaged, laughing and entertained, but also had a message. You were the highlight of my meeting!"

Cindy Ferguson
Certified Exhibition Manager
Director of Marketing, APRO

■ ■ ■

"Before I stand to speak to my leadership classes now, I immediately empty my pockets, take off my watch, and set it to the side. I am much more aware of keeping my hands out of my pockets, even in casual conversations. Moreover, the high level of participation from some of our more bashful employees was truly fun and exciting to watch."

Donnie Bond
Learning and Performance Specialist
Coast Electric Power Association

■ ■ ■

"The topics you presented received exceptionally high praise. The first was The No-Panic Checklist. This checklist is a tremendous tool to use in preparation for a presentation. And, the Three-Minute First Impression rule was a good reminder for even the seasoned speakers in the group."

Robert Kirkland
Business Development Officer and Manager
Technology Transfer and Communications
Center for Advanced Vehicular Systems

■ ■ ■

"I did my first presentation last Thursday. Mandi, thanks to you, the presentation went beautifully and I passed with flying colors. My colleagues were very impressed. Thanks again."

Sunja E. Stuckey
First Vice President of Business Development
BancorpSouth

"It was loaded with relevant and practical tools that we can put to use immediately. Our officers are still enthusiastically talking about the things they learned from you. Two people have reported that they have already put some of their new skills to work."

David H. Hoster II
President and CEO
EastGroup Properties

■ ■ ■

"The other big idea we've acted upon is moving up our internal deadline for job interview presentations by one day. This gives us a full day of rehearsal where we can work on the little things that make a big difference. You heightened our awareness of the filler words (basically, actually, uh, um), our body language, and specifically 'speaker's stance.' Best of all, just today I was in a presentation planning meeting when one of our principals declined using slides for an upcoming interview—an unheard of practice before your visit. As a group, we are seeing the value of sharing our message with powerful, well-organized and interactive dialogue rather than relying on slides to hit the high points. The light bulbs continue to click!"

Tamara Goff
Director of Marketing
Hnedak Bobo Group

■ ■ ■

"Here's the tip I learned: to think of the room in quadrants during a speech so that you don't favor one side of the room or even one particular person. We even watched you model that during the program. Thanks for sharing with us."

Sue Lichtenstein
Membership Director
La Cima Club, Irving, Texas

■ ■ ■

"Our delegates learned from the content, which some already have started to implement in their daily operation. Guiding us to use the mapping process and making sure we keep eye contact with our audiences helped us raise our standards in communication."

Francis Vlok
Director of Human Resources and Customer Service
Sprint Mart

"Everyone had positive things to say and the best part of all—
they have adapted their skills. I have noticed since your presentation
that my leasing teams are standing and greeting the prospects
differently. I haven't seen a 'lobster pincher' handshake since
June. It is great to see my team grow in a positive direction."

Patty Price
Regional Property Manager
LEDIC Management Group, Inc.

■ ■ ■

"Our members are already putting your good advice to work. We had
lots of very, very positive feedback, and I personally got so much out of
it. I used your techniques on a proposal last week and couldn't believe
how much I caught by really focusing on the words. I also used the
mapping approach to put together a mission statement for one of my
clients, and that technique made it so much easier for me to consider
all of the angles. I wish I had known this method years ago."

Amy D. Nolan, APR
President
Public Relations Association of Louisiana, Baton Rouge Chapter

■ ■ ■

"What struck me is the story of how you designed an entire presentation
while stuck in a traffic jam. For me that really drove home the
importance of planning and preparation—and how we should never
wait and just try to do a presentation 'off the top of our head.'"

Angie Bittle
Learning and Development Training Specialist
Duke Energy Corporation

■ ■ ■

"This book looks cool. Did you really write it?"

Rett Stanley
Mandi's seven-year-old son

The
NO-PANIC
PLAN
for Presenters

An A-to-Z Checklist for Speaking Confidently
and Compellingly Anywhere, Anytime

Mandi Stanley 2013

Mandi Stanley
Certified Speaking Professional

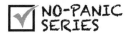
NO-PANIC
SERIES

Pecan Row Press

Jackson, Mississippi

The No-Panic Plan for Presenters
An A-to-Z Checklist for Speaking Confidently and Compellingly Anywhere, Anytime

Copyright © 2011 by Mandi Stanley

International Standard Book Number: 978-0-9795187-3-7
Library of Congress Catalog Number: 2010938228

Library of Congress Cataloging-in-Publication data
Stanley, Mandi
The No-Panic Plan for Presenters / written by Mandi Stanley
    1. Business Reference. 2. Communications
    I. Stanley, Mandi. II. Title

Printed in the United States of America

Order information. Pecan Row Press titles may be purchased in bulk for business, educational, fundraising, or sales promotional use. For information, please e-mail info@pecanrowpress.com.

The No-Panic Plan for Presenters by Mandi Stanley, CSP, denotes a series of resources that may include but is not limited to books, mini e-courses, pocket flip charts, checklists, CDs, and interactive DVDs.

Pecan Row Press
603 Duling Avenue, Suite 202
Jackson, Mississippi 39216
www.pecanrowpress.com

Dedication

To **Dr. Denise Dudley**,
who saw something in me I never saw in myself
back in 1995 and single-handedly encouraged
and launched my speaking career.
What a risk taker!

To **Dr. Jimmy W. Abraham**,
executive director, Mississippi State University Alumni
Association, who taught a group of 19 orientation
leaders the true meaning of unconditional love
during the summer of 1990—and equipped us
with the skill of making presentations
while walking backward down the sidewalk.

To **Judy and Larry Marett**, my parents,
who taught me to double check.

And to **Bob Stanley**,
who asked me to marry him 20 years ago.
He was the real risk taker!

You all have left indelible imprints on my life.
Dedicating this book is just one little way
I know how to say "thank you."

NO-PANIC
Contents

"In the jungle of public speaking, in the end it's not the lion or the tiger that eats you alive—it's the *mosquito*. The smallest details make the biggest difference."

Mandi Stanley, CSP

Motivation for
The
NO-PANIC PLAN
for Presenters

To-do lists.

The mere concept sends business professionals diving into two diverse camps. First are the individuals who practically salivate with glee at the thought of checking off another item from their daily color-coded lists of projects to accomplish—in order, of course. They prepare the next day's list the night before and probably have similar lists and calendars for each member of their household. Simply put, they love their lists and would be lost without them. They depend on their personal hand-held device to tell them what to do and where to go and what time to be there. Their lives would come to an abrupt stop if they ever lost their daily planner. And they wouldn't dream of entering the supermarket without a shopping list in aisle-by-aisle order.

Then, you have the folks who run kicking and screaming from any constricting to-do list. Having to organize their plans and projects for the day in some left-brained format would result in unfortunate erratic twitching. They wing it, and it works well for them. Of course, their grocery bills are twice as much as they should be because they don't carry a shopping list to the store and end up wondering later, "Why did I buy this?"

While many professionals have a love-hate relationship with their task lists, checklists, and even shopping lists, I tend toward the love side.

Indeed, I depend on lists for everything, and they certainly help both my business and household run more smoothly.

When it comes to traveling for business, I rely upon three lists for a successful trip.

The first is my packing list.

Even though I have been traveling full time on the seminar circuit for more than 15 years—and packing the same suitcases for most of those years—there's always the possibility of forgetting my toothbrush, or antiperspirant, or even my shoes. That's why I still pull out the checklist every time to double check. That's probably also why it's time I purchase new luggage!

The second is my briefcase/toolkit packing list for my actual presentation.

It includes reminders to pack my portable lavaliere microphone, extra batteries, laptop, presentation software, handout masters, back-up copies, and various props and door prizes. Missing or forgetting any of these items would have negative repercussions on my overall message.

The third is what brings us here today.

It is a special checklist I've developed throughout years of experience as a corporate trainer and executive speaking coach. It is a checklist for content and delivery.

When I work one on one with executive speakers, sales representatives, members of the clergy, candidates running for public office, and other politicians, I provide them with a typed-out list of reminders. They are instructed to review it thoroughly 48 hours before their upcoming talk or speech. It includes practical advice such as:

- What your first sentence should achieve
- The must-have elements of the opening three minutes
- How to reinforce your sticking points throughout the speech

- How to guarantee a strong closing
- Tips about eye contact, gestures, and more

I use the same list myself. I review it on the airplane on my way to speak at a conference. I casually have referred to it as a "no-panic" checklist for presenters and have demonstrated to my clients how to use it successfully.

As you may have guessed, throughout the years several of my clients and friends have mentioned in passing, "You know, you should consider publishing this." Deep down, I always questioned if people would want to read something I had written. After all, this began as a little handwritten checklist so I wouldn't forget anything. Would other presenters really find this as useful and user friendly as I do? After several years of prodding and coaxing, my friends, clients, and even some of my audience members convinced me to do it.

So, what you are holding right now is an updated and better version of the same tool I've used for more than a decade. To make *The No-Panic Plan for Presenters* work for you, you can approach it two ways.

The TSA won't let you board a commercial flight with a laser pointer in your possession. I should know: I've had to "donate" mine to the friendly airport security agent not once, but twice.

First, peruse these pages 48 hours before a big speech or presentation. Reproduce and use the actual checklists inside. For instance, make sure you can answer the essential questions about your audience's make-up. Run through the hints to make sure you're not too long-winded! Double check that you've packed your laser pointer. Of course, these days it is better to make sure you have a laser pointer available on site. The TSA won't let you board a commercial flight with one in your possession. I should know: I've had to "donate" mine to the friendly airport security agent not once, but twice. Expensive lesson learned.

Second, once or twice a year, read through these pages to make sure your content and delivery are the best they possibly can be every time the spotlight is on you.

There are thousands of texts published on the topic of professional presentation skills. What differentiates this one is the abundance of presentation checklists. I even have included a room-cleaning checklist for the end of your presentation. After all, we should attempt to leave any place we go better than we found it, even the meeting room. These lists are designed to cut your prep time significantly and avert forgetfulness.

■ ■ ■

A wise woman from Amory, Mississippi, once gave me some advice I'll never forget.

It's one of those catchy Southern sayings that just kind of sticks with you through the years:

"In the jungle of life, in the end, it's not the lion or the tiger that eats you alive—it's the *mosquito*."

Homespun, but how true.

At the time I had just graduated from college and was heading out to the big city of Dallas. Her encouragement was to keep my faith and stay true not just in the big decisions but also in the small daily challenges of life that can make or break us. Success—or failure for that matter—is found in the details, the daily decisions that shape and mold us.

I even have included a room-cleaning checklist for the end of your presentation. After all, we should attempt to leave any place we go better than we found it, even the meeting room.

Likewise, I believe the same can be said for those of us called upon to speak or present to a group of people: the little details make a big difference. It can be either one of the most terrifying or the most rewarding experiences of your life. You can know your content cold, but don't forget up to *93 percent* of your message comes from your eye contact, body movement, vocal tone, gestures, posture, filler phrases, even your clothing, hair, and shoes. Even if you know what you're going to say, awareness of the other elements involved will prevent you from sending your audience distracting mixed messages.

So, before you hit the stage, before you approach the podium, before you open your mouth, remember:

"In this jungle we call *public speaking*, in the end, it's not the lion or the tiger that eats you alive—it's the mosquito."

Please consider **The No-Panic Plan for Presenters** to be the ideal tool to rid your next presentation of any pesky problems.

Interspersed throughout the text are sections labeled **Ouch! Lesson Learned the Hard Way.** Someone once quipped that "A wise man learns from his mistakes; an even wiser man learns from someone else's mistakes." Apparently, I'm not the "wiser man" in several speaking scenarios because I have blown it—*really* blown it—so many times. Yet, my most drastic presentation improvements have been born of pain—the pain of totally messing up or not paying enough attention to some of my own speaking "mosquitoes." I have learned more from my mistakes than my speaking successes—or at least I remember the mistakes more vividly—and I have included these stories so that you may have the benefit of learning from my mistakes instead of your own.

Here's to your next standing ovation!

The success of your next presentation depends on your ability to connect with your audience. It's all about them, not you.

"Where you stand on an issue often depends on where you sit."
The Tongue and Quill

■ ■ ■

"A good listener is not only popular everywhere,
but after a while, he gets to know something."
Wilson Miner

■ ■ ■

"We are given one tongue, but two ears that we may
hear from others twice as much as we speak."
Epictetus

■ ■ ■

"You have two ears and one mouth.
Use them in that proportion."
Mrs. Eleanor Slaughter
Distinguished Delta Gamma alumna

■ ■ ■

"It seems rather incongruous that in a society of
super-sophisticated communication,
we often suffer from a shortage of listeners."
Erma Bombeck

■ ■ ■

"It's not about you."
Rick Warren

A

Analyze Your Audience

ONE DAY Robert, a forty-something sales representative, received a call from his regional manager.

"Robert, we need you to say a few words about territorial management at the annual kick-off meeting in Chicago next week. Just 20 minutes or so—that's all. We want you to talk about how you achieved 108 percent of your business plan and some of the time management systems you used to make your number this year."

With that directive from his boss, Robert ran down the hall to his office, closed the door, had a seat, and immediately buried his head in his computer for the next four hours. What was he doing? Why, creating his PowerPoint® presentation, of course!

That's what happens with so many executive speakers I encounter. As soon as they are given the time and date of their next presentation or meeting, they rush to the computer and start with the slides.

Wrong first step.

The slides are not the presentation. PowerPoint® and similar programs such as Keynote® are visual *aids*, with emphasis on the word *aid*. Such visuals should be used to complement the main points of your presentation, not *be* your presentation. As far as I know, no one has been moved to a climatic emotional decision because of a bulleted list on a PowerPoint® slide. Yet, I've worked with numerous presenters who have attempted to cram 83 slides into a 20-minute presentation. With the exception of the famed *National Geographic* photographer and conference keynoter Dewitt Jones, whose breathtaking and awe-inspiring slideshows always elicit "oohs" and "aahs" from his audiences, do you really know of anyone who has walked into a business meeting and said, "I can't wait to see this speaker's slides"?

Some speaking and training consultants assert that PowerPoint® is not the presentation; instead, *you* are the presentation. While I understand that reasoning, I contend it's not so much you but rather *your audience* who is the presentation. And if that doesn't quite resonate with you, remember: The success of your next presentation depends on your ability to connect with your audience. It's all about them, not you. Before you start scripting out what you are going to say, or deciding which animation to use for your slides, ask first who's going to be listening to your message. Who is your target? Who is your end user, so to speak? There is a certain art to your audience analysis.

Can you answer these crucial questions about the audience before each presentation? Some of your answers will be quite general in nature and involve a wide range. Others will be exact.

■ General educational background of those in attendance?
■ Job titles and work responsibilities?
■ Knowledge level of your topic?
■ Number of people expected?
■ Age range?

- Gender?
- Geographical location/culture?
- Attitude and interest level?
- "Hot buttons" or taboo subjects?

General educational background of those in attendance

What level of school have most completed? High school graduates? College education? Or do most people have graduate degrees?

You don't want to speak at a level above the heads of the people in attendance. If they don't understand you, rather than asking clarifying questions, they'll just tune you out and not really hear anything you have to say. You'll become background noise much akin to the unseen teacher in Charlie Brown's classroom: "Whah whaaa, whah whaaa, whah, whaaa." At the same time, you don't want to water down or "dumb down" your message to a level that is insulting to others.

Job titles and work responsibilities

What do they have in common work wise? Do they work in an industry laden with acronyms and abbreviations? Will they understand the industry-specific terms you'll be using? Should you define them first, or does everyone know what they mean? Could it potentially be a source of confusion?

You'll become background noise much akin to the unseen teacher in Charlie Brown's classroom: "Whah whaaa, whah whaaa, whah, whaaa."

One woman attending an insurance workshop in Colorado received the detailed conference brochure well in advance of the meeting. Along with the travel recommendations, meeting agenda, and even the menu, the brochure described how "... reasonable accommodations have been made in all meeting facilities in accordance with ADA requirements." A bit puzzled by that detail, she called the conference hotline to ask, "Could you tell me what in the world the American *Dairy* Association has to do with our meeting?"

ADA in that instance meant Americans with Disabilities Act, and it illustrates why no acronym should be assumed a no-brainer.

Consider FYI, for an example. A few years back I mailed some baby pictures of my first-born son to my in-laws. They didn't own a computer and had no access to e-mail or the World Wide Web, so I made a special effort to print extra copies of photos to send to them. In fact, I mailed them photos almost every week. With this particular batch of baby shots, I had included a sticky note which read, "FYI: These are pics of Rett at three days old leaving the hospital." A couple of days later, Bob and I received a phone call from his mom. She said, "We've been thinking about it and thinking about it, and we've finally figured out what FYI means: From Your In-laws!"

Knowledge level of your topic
Again, will they be familiar with certain projects you address, case studies you cite, and the jargon you may use?

Number of people expected
Are you preparing for 12 or 120? It makes a difference, even down to the visuals you use, the interactive techniques you employ, the audiovisual equipment you require, and perhaps the clothes you wear. The number of audience members also affects the timing of your talk. The larger the crowd, usually the more cushion time you build in.

Age range
Have you noticed your audiences are getting younger and younger? Truly though, are most of your typical audience members considered to be baby boomers? Their expectations of your delivery differ from those of the next generational group. This next group is the Sesame Street® crowd, people who grew up watching the show and who now expect a bit more creativity and even pizzazz in your presentation style. Then, of course, the next group of professionals in the workforce today has never known a world without MTV®. They really do expect more "bells and whistles," even in a business presentation. After all, you don't want

them sitting in the back row watching clips from the latest viral videos on their cell phones while you are droning away up front.

Gender

Yes, usually there is a mix of male and female audience members. Answering this question, however, can influence examples you use. The primary makeup of your audience even can determine how you dress for a speech. I know I am more apt to wear pantsuits and darker colors when addressing a primarily male audience and will wear brighter and more festive colors if I'm speaking at a women's conference. That's just a personal preference, but it's still a consideration.

Geographical location/culture

This is a question worth researching and exploring if you are speaking internationally. Even if you are presenting in the United States or your native country, are there special references or other facts to consider depending on the region? How do you pronounce the word *pecan*? Or *envelope*? Are you certain you are pronouncing their city, county, and province names correctly? This is good to keep in mind if you ever travel to Olathe, Kansas, or Pullyallup, Washington. My husband personally witnessed a sales representative from Omaha travel throughout northeast Mississippi just butchering some of the town pronunciations there. Needless to say, he didn't win many friends or influence many people while traveling in the area. For example, a little homework was all he needed to know locals pronounce Amory as the two-syllable "AIM-ree," not "am-uh-REE."

After all, you don't want them in the back row watching funny video clips on their cell phones while you're droning away up front.

Attitude and interest level

Are they happy to be with you? Are they there by choice? Did they pay to hear you speak? Do they support your platform or topic? Or, are they a more neutral crowd? Are they just curious about what you have to say? Is it a tough crowd? An angry mob? Was it mandatory they attend? Did someone else tell them they had to be there? Are you there to deliver bad news to good people? Those presentations are never easy. Proactively asking questions such as these sometimes will help you "expect the unexpected" and truly shine if dealing with a difficult participant or complicated situation.

"Hot buttons" or taboo subjects

Think about these and any other references before you stand up and speak. Be sure to discuss any off-limits topics with the meeting planner or event organizer prior to your presentation.

This is not a time to "fake it until you make it."

For example, has there been a recent downsizing? Have they just switched to a new computer software system that is driving everyone nuts? The higher-ups may not want you to mention it, even jokingly. Has there been a recent death within the company you should know about?

Let's face it: We've all been in audiences where the speakers have failed to do their homework. It doesn't take long to figure that out. This is not a time to "fake it until you make it." Sometimes it's simply a case of being the wrong speaker with the wrong message for that audience on that given day. Perhaps you've sat through career interviews where you can tell the applicant hasn't bothered to conduct homework on the company, the job, or even the interviewing committee.

One other benefit of doing homework on your audience is figuratively to seat yourself in their chairs, thereby becoming more aware of big audience turnoffs. Speakers who engage in the art of audience analysis are less likely to be the target of these complaints:

- Too long winded
- Took too long to get to the point
- Too much fluff and filler
- Used too many weird acronyms
- Seemed arrogant

- Came across as a know-it-all
- "Chased rabbits around the room"
- Used too many annoying vocal fillers
- Too monotone
- Poor attempts at humor

Generally speaking, your audience is just like you. Ask yourself: What else is on their minds right now? What were they doing prior to entering the room? With whom did they just talk on their cell phone? What did they have for breakfast? Are they preoccupied with familial issues, tight deadlines, even the weather forecast?

Audience analysis ensures a closer connection with those who need to hear your message most.

And on a lighter note, FYI means "For Your Information," just in case you're wondering.

I submit you really are not ready to speak in front of any group unless you at least know the basic answers to these nine questions. Some of the answers will be extremely general or include a range. That's okay. Just realize you may not necessarily be qualified to speak if you don't know some of the answers. After all, you don't want to end up being the wrong speaker with the wrong message for your audience on that particular day. Make some phone calls. Ask some questions. Take the time to connect with your audience.

There's a difference between preparing for eight people gathered in a conference room versus 500 in an auditorium.

There's a difference between preparing for eight people gathered in a conference room versus 500 in an auditorium. Knowing the basic backgrounds of people prevents you from using unfamiliar acronyms and speaking over their heads or "dumbing down" your message and insulting somebody in attendance. Knowing your audience makeup and the ages represented even can determine what to wear when presenting and which visual aids you choose.

Now what?

Well before your presentation date, fill out the ***Audience Analysis Checklist***. Use this one as a guideline to customize and create your own. After all, it's all about your audience.

The **NO-PANIC PLAN** *for Presenters*

 Audience Analysis Checklist

❑ Title of presentation: _____

❑ Time & length of session: _____

❑ Date of presentation: _____

❑ Objective of presentation: _____
_____

❑ Number of people expected: _____

❑ Age range: _____

❑ Is my audience gender specific?_____

❑ General educational background: _____

❑ Job titles and work responsibilities: _____
_____

❑ How familiar with topic? _____

❑ Geographical location and cultural considerations: _____
_____

❑ Attitude and interest level (realistically): _____
_____

❑ Any "hot buttons" or taboo topics to avoid? _____
_____

❑ What questions are they likely to have about my topic? _____
_____
_____

Follow-Up Actions

As a result of this presentation, my audience will _____
_____

"Be prepared. Be interesting. Be brief. Be seated!"
Training manager
American Management Association International

■ ■ ■

"There is nothing wrong with having nothing to say—
unless you insist on saying it."
Unknown

B

Believe the Four B's of Public Speaking

FOR FIVE YEARS I served on the faculty of the American Management Association International, traveling and teaching one-day seminars for their Padgett-Thompson and Keye Productivity Center divisions. I worked on the five-cities-in-five-days circuit. For example, Monday might find me in Denver; Tuesday in Salt Lake City; Wednesday in Boise; Thursday in Seattle; and Friday in Portland, Oregon. A trainer could start the week in Jacksonville, Florida, and drive south along the coast stopping in Orlando, West Palm Beach, and Fort Lauderdale before wrapping up the week in Miami. To prepare us for what was sometimes a grueling and definitely jam-packed traveling and speaking schedule, new trainers were required to complete an intense two-week orientation. My training manager and orientation leader at the time shared some of the best advice I received early in my career as a professional speaker. It was a takeoff on the old

Franklin D. Roosevelt one-liner: "Be sincere; be brief; be seated," and it's as simple as this:

<u>Be</u> prepared
<u>Be</u> interesting
<u>Be</u> brief
<u>Be</u> seated!

He said that was the ultimate secret to being well received and producing a successful seminar. Certainly, it's the key to running a successful and productive business meeting as well.

Take an honest assessment: Do you like to hear yourself talk? Many executive speakers do. Do you know people who tend to go on just a little too long, maybe 10 or 15 minutes after they should have wrapped

Some speakers just don't know when to stop.

things up? It's a common tendency of many presenters. Think about it from the listener's perspective: Have you ever sat in the audience and thought, "Okay. Enough's enough. You've already said that; you're just repeating yourself now. Stick a fork in it; you're done!" You lean to your next-seat neighbor and whisper, "Her presentation was really good—if she had just stopped 10 minutes ago." Some speakers just don't know when to stop.

Now what?

If you are given 20 minutes to speak, time it. Don't guess. If you are given five minutes, time it twice. Five minutes can stretch into 10 minutes all too easily.

If you are speaking at a professional conference and are given 60 minutes for your break-out session, prepare a 50-minute presentation. Give yourself that extra cushion time to account for your introducer, possible technical glitches, generous laughter after your jokes, and of course, your standing ovation at the end.

OUCH! Lesson Learned the Hard Way

On a personal note, I'm a stickler for punctuality and timeliness. In fact, I was hired for my first job fresh out of college because I was punctual. I've been speaking professionally full time since 1995, and only twice have I exceeded my targeted ending time. However, I recall the first time vividly because I truly lost sleep over it. It was in Albany, New York, in the middle of a blizzard. The severe weather had pushed everything back, but I still had seven people show up for the seminar, so the show had to go on. I was supposed to end at 4 p.m., and I finished at 4:20. It was so obvious the attendees were preoccupied with the weather and were anxious to go home, but I foolishly was determined to complete every learning objective we had promised in the brochure. What should I have done differently to manage my time— and my audience's time—better? We had started the program late, but that was no excuse. I should have adjusted and ended at the promised time. I determined it would never happen again, blizzard or no blizzard!

Good advice: Always leave them longing for more.

Unfortunately, the second occurrence was just last year with an audience of 25 nuclear engineers on a tight schedule. We went seven minutes past the allotted time because people had numerous questions. Some people wouldn't consider that as running late, but I'm clock watcher, and apparently several people in my audience were as well and complained about it on their evaluations. I should have facilitated the Q & A portion better.

Here's the point: *Never, never, never go overtime.* It's disrespectful to your audience, and time is a precious commodity along the lines of money, energy, and creativity. They have chosen to invest their time with you, be it 30 minutes, two hours, or a full day. Speakers must respect that investment of time and not abuse it.

Good advice: *Always leave them longing for more.*

As I learned in Albany, unexpected events may force you to do some on-the-spot adjustments to stay on schedule. So pull out that stopwatch now. Please be aware that any written presentation will take longer to deliver than it appears on paper. Typically, one typed page equals two minutes of spoken delivery.

Allow me to share two approaches to timing your presentation.

First, many executive speakers time their talks slide by slide. Power-Point® and Keynote® provide users with an automatic timer to click and record timing down to the second. Using the presenter's view screen on the computer while the actual slideshow projects on the big screen allows the speaker to keep an eye on the timing and stay on track. The presenter's view screen also features a large notes section and a sneak peek at the next slide in order. It's quite a user-friendly tool.

Second, and this is my approach, is to time your presentation point by point. For example, I color code my notes on paper. I use black for my basic outline and main points, blue for anecdotes, green for interactives, and red to signal any props, visual aids, and slide transitions. I then walk through the presentation and use a yellow highlighter in the margin to indicate the time per point. It may look something like this:

Action versus information explanation (black)	4 minutes
List of acronyms to avoid (red)	1 minute
Story of in-laws and FYI (blue)	2 minutes
Practice writing exercise for acronyms and jargon (green)	5 minutes

That module from my ***Ten Fast Writing Tips for Executives*** seminar takes 12 minutes. You now can see how easy it is for me to know what to cut if the meeting starts late. I simply can omit the personal anecdote about my in-laws to save two minutes and gain some extra time, even though I love that story, and the audience always laughs.

Timing is everything.

Be prepared. Be interesting. Be brief. And then, be seated.

✓ NO-PANIC Notes

Confidence begins in the eye of the beholder.

"The only one who can tell you 'you can't'
is you. And you don't have to listen."
Nike advertisement

■ ■ ■

"Whatever people think, is."
Otis Singletary

Close with Conviction

WE CAN GO "C CRAZY" with closings. Closings should be concise, controlled, clear, and complimentary as appropriate; should circle back to the beginning; and even could involve handing out certificates and the collection of evaluations. We had seminar auditors pop in unannounced at our one-day classes, and they would monitor our closing statements to meet the seminar company's guidelines on this checklist of C's. I nicknamed them the Seven C's, and the moniker stuck. We were expected to sail the closing Seven C's smoothly.

Basically there are two categories of presentations: action presentations and information presentations. Your purpose determines your closing.

Action presentations
Action presentations are developed around the questions: "What do I want my audience to do?" "How do I want my audience to feel?" An action presentation is written and presented because you want your

recipients to do something as a result of hearing it or to act in some way differently as a result of being there. Sales presentations, persuasive talks, motivational programs, and even pep talks from coaches in the team locker room are action presentations.

Information presentations

Information presentations answer the question: "What do I want my audience to know?" Presenters don't necessarily want their audience members to go out and *do* something as a result of hearing what they have to say. They simply want their target audience to *know* something they perhaps didn't know about before, or they want them to *understand* a subject better. True informational presentations center on the classic lead sentence. The lead sentence answers the six journalist's questions, the five W's and the one H: the *who, what, when, where, why,* and *how.*

Your first step as a presenter is to ask yourself: Is this an *action presentation* or an *information presentation?* The answer to that one question alone determines how you tailor your message to your audience and how you close it.

Even pep talks from coaches in the team locker room are action presentations. Usually someone in a seminar will ask, "Can a presentation be both an action-oriented and an informational presentation?" The answer is *yes.* But, if it is both action and information, ultimately how should we treat it? We treat it as an *action* presentation. We may be providing our audiences with a lot of information, but we do so in hopes they will choose a wise course of action, and we define that as the ultimate goal of our presentation.

With the answer to that question, surprisingly most professional speakers craft their closing statement first. That's right: They write their ending first. There's a communication principle known as the Law of Primacy and Recency. People remember best what they hear first and last; therefore, first and last are critical locations for key memorable information. Recency refers to the last main idea you want floating around in the heads of your meeting attendees as they exit the room.

If it is an action presentation, your closing statement is your call to action. Many speakers plan to use emotion in the closings of their action presentations. The call to action may include a deadline or target date for response. Motivational speakers try to invoke a future challenge. Sales presenters use the closing to review the next steps, usually for ordering or buying. This requires careful planning and exact wording.

For information presentations, the closing is the summary statement. Think of it as the executive summary. You highlight the main points and circle back to the lead sentence. Therefore, your lead sentence serves as your beginning and your end. For informational presentations, consider the old military writing techniques of BLUF and BLAB. BLUF stands for Bottom Line Up Front, and the closing is the BLAB: Bottom Line At Bottom. Yes, this is one time when it actually is good to BLAB during a speech.

Regardless if it's an action presentation or an information presentation, check your conclusion for three necessary elements. When I work one on one with executive presenters, we review their closings on video to identify these three components of a strong ending. I never want any of my clients simply to sputter out at the end or drone on into oblivion. As Joe Calloway, a member of the Speaker Hall of Fame, describes it: "You don't want to just meander into nothingness and wander off the stage." We love a good ending. We love a happy ending. Our audience just wants a strong ending, period. So, dissect in order:

1. The closing signal
2. The summary statement
3. The big bang

The closing signal
Audiences perk up at closing signals such as:

"In conclusion..."

"To wrap things up today..."
"So I leave you with this challenge..."
"I'll end with one last example of..."

Include a transitional phrase such as one of these as you move to your closing.

The summary statement

Can you summarize your message in one key sentence? Make sure people understand your message and are clear on their next steps as a result. For an informational presentation, your summary sentence is a version of your lead sentence repeated at the end. Some people view this as the executive summary. For an action-oriented presentation, the summary usually is a final call to action with important deadlines attached.

The big bang

Here are some tried-and-true ideas for the big bang. Consider these attention grabbers as you purposefully craft your presentation's closing:

- Ending with questions that challenge your participants
- Using a final personal anecdote or good story you have saved for the end
- Finishing with a short yet meaningful quotation
- Using one last bold fact or startling statistic
- Repeating the one big idea
- Relating your main point to a current newsworthy event
- Invoking your call to action
- Creatively circling back to your opening statements
- Tying everything together with a fitting and well-planned analogy

I even end one of my presentations with a magic trick. People remember it. All things being equal, a strong creative closing could be the portion of your presentation that sets you apart from the crowd, simply because you took the time to plan it.

Unfortunately, some speakers don't really think about their last words. They haven't really considered the ending. They don't plan or script out their closing. The entire speech can fall flat as a result. Strong, well-planned closing statements separate professional speakers from amateurs. Below are some of the most common closing mistakes I see executive speakers commit. These are true closing clunkers:

- Fizzling out at the end
- Saving Q&A for the very end
- Packing up materials while still speaking and making closing comments
- Apologizing for anything
- Promising a false ending
- Not ending on time
- Failing to thank the audience

Fizzling out at the end

We've all seen this happen in business meetings. A speaker hasn't practiced how to close, so he or she says something along the lines of, "Well, I guess that's it. Any questions?" "Oh, it looks as if we're out of time, unless you have any questions." They seemingly add this as an afterthought and appear to hope no one asks any questions. This is implied through their lack of eye contact with the audience, speaking at a lower volume, and hurrying back to their seats without strategically "handing the baton" to the next speaker or the facilitator. Some unprepared speakers even say, "Well, I guess that's all I have to say," and just shrink back to their seats. Don't let this happen to you.

Saving Q&A for the very end

At professional conferences, the question-and-answer session is an important portion of many presentations. I've spoken at conferences where it was mandatory to save time for questions from the audience, and the allotted time can be anywhere from five minutes to sometimes 30 minutes. However, it should not be the final element of your speech. I repeat: It should not be the final element of your speech. You, the presenter, must have the final word for a strong memorable closing. There-fore, after the last main point, provide a transition to open the floor for questions, repeat the question asked so everyone in the room can hear and understand it, answer the question truthfully and to your best abil-ity, watch the time, say you have time for one final question, and after the last question, close with your final planned remarks. What's the last idea you want floating around in their minds as they leave? It's not typically some random question someone in your audience has asked. It should be your big bang.

Facilitate Q&A smoothly by following this process:
1. After the last main point, provide a transition to open the floor for questions
2. Repeat the question asked so everyone in the room can hear and understand it
3. Answer the question truthfully and to your best ability
4. Watch the time
5. Say you have time for one final question
6. After answering the last question, close with your final remarks

Packing up materials while still speaking and making closing comments

Oops, I've been nailed on this one before. It's a bad habit. I also have the annoying habit of clearing the dinner table while some people are still eating. The lesson: Wait until you have completely finished your comments to turn off your laptop and tuck your notes into your brief-case. Otherwise, you are communicating to the people listening to you that you've already said anything worth hearing, so maybe they should tune you out and begin packing up their notes, too.

Apologizing for anything

It's just a good idea to remind yourself that your audience probably hasn't seen a written copy of your presentation or speech. They won't know if you accidentally forgot a story, unless you regress and tell them. They probably won't even know if you left out a key point.

OUCH! Lesson Learned the Hard Way

For example, in *No-Panic Presentation Skills* seminars, I place a small piece of chocolate wrapped in gold paper at each seat. The candy has a specific purpose, and I explain it about 10 minutes into the presentation. However, at a recent women's conference in Louisiana, I totally forgot to tell them about the chocolate, and I didn't realize I had not mentioned it until the end when I noticed no one had touched the chocolate. It's usually gobbled up halfway through the program. How could I forget such a key element in a presentation I conduct 30 times a year? It happens. Of course, no one in my audience that day knew any better. They didn't think twice about the chocolate. They probably just gathered it up with their learning guides and were happy to have a little snack on the way home! I kicked myself, but I never said a word.

Promising a false ending

We've seen it countless times. An executive speaker starts to conclude, even signals the audience with the words "in closing," yet decides to tell another story or go back to a previous point or even introduce new information. And then, she'll end again by saying, "So in conclusion," and repeat the vicious cycle. A running joke among some preachers in churches is that "in conclusion," really means we have another good 20 minutes left! Of course, the congregation expects the sermon to be wrapped up quickly so they can head out to lunch.

Don't lie to your audience. When you signal the ending, they expect it. Many times, they are looking forward to it. When you say it's your one final thought, make it your one final thought. Say it and stop. Anything you add after you've begun closing lessens the strength of your final point.

Not ending on time

This shows a lack of respect for your audience and other presenters. Unfortunately, it is a common tendency, and I might add a problem, among many high-level executives. I've personally witnessed a business leader take almost one hour when he was scheduled on the agenda for 15 minutes. He totally destroyed the schedule for the meeting, and he ate into the next two speakers' times. Stop on time. Your audience will respect you more as a result, and to date, I've never heard of anyone complain about someone who gave a speech that was too short.

Failing to thank your audience

Yes, I know some speaking coaches admonish never thank an audience because they should be the ones thanking you. If I were 10 years old, I'd say, "Puh-leeze." I've never bought into this advice. Most certainly, it *is* appropriate to thank your audience; after all, they have invested a top commodity in you: their time. To many people these days, time may be considered a more valuable asset than money. But be specific in your thanks. On what grounds should you thank your audience?

> **There's nothing taboo about offering your audience a sincere thank you. You'll end on a positive note every time.**

- Obviously, for their investment of time
- For the invitation to speak to them in the first place
- As former National Speakers Association President Naomi Rhode, CSP, CPAE, would say, for the "privilege of the platform"
- For their hospitality
- For their interaction with you and their willingness to share ideas
- For asking meaningful questions

There's nothing taboo about offering your audience a sincere thank you. You'll end on a positive note every time.

Now what?

- First, determine if your next presentation can be categorized as an *action* or *information* presentation. What do you ultimately want to achieve? If it is an action presentation, end with your call to action and any associated deadlines or future steps. If it is an information presentation, close with your summary statement to bring the presentation full circle.

- Choose among the recommended closing clinchers as you rehearse your big bang.
- Write out your closing statement word for word. Script it and work on it so you can close with great eye contact and without looking at your notes.

The NO-PANIC PLAN *for Presenters*

 Closing with Conviction Checklist

Must Do's in the Closing

The closing signal

Write your closing signal here: _____

_____

The summary statement or call to action

Script out your summary statement here: _____

_____

The big bang

Describe your closing big bang here. Perhaps choose from this list:

❏ Ending with questions that challenge your participants

❏ Using a final personal anecdote or good story you have saved for the end

❏ Finishing with a short yet meaningful quotation

❏ Using one last bold fact or startling statistic

❏ Repeating the one big idea

❏ Relating your main point to a current newsworthy event

❏ Invoking your call to action

❏ Creatively circling back to your opening statements

❏ Tying everything together with a fitting and well-planned analogy

_____

_____

Avoid falling victim to any of these *closing clunkers:*
- Fizzling out at the end
- Saving Q&A for the very end
- Packing up materials while still speaking and making closing comments
- Apologizing for anything
- Promising a false ending
- Not ending on time
- Failing to thank the audience

BONUS: C

Create Confidence

As you speak, so are you perceived, and you eventually become. If you speak with confidence, you are perceived as confident, and you become more confident.

These nonverbal cues let your audience know you believe in what you are saying and doing. Confidence begins in the eye of the beholder. Professional speakers know these secrets to looking confident, even when they're not. Here's a hint: It's the same advice your mother gave you. So, check the mirror before you go on stage, and remember:

- Stand up straight
- Smile
- Make natural eye contact
- Let go of anything you are holding that shows you have "the shakes"
- Be yourself
- Don't forget to breathe

Now what?

Here are a few homework assignments to bolster your confidence:

Rehearse in the room
Some people call this a dry run. Others call it a run-through. Still others refer to it as an actual dress rehearsal.

Well before the audience arrives, get into the meeting room if possible. Take the stage, look out across the room, set your notes on the lectern, turn on the microphone, and hear yourself say a few words. Work with the audio-visual staff to run through your visual presentation, verifying it is in sync with the projector and that you are comfortable using the remote. Make sure the projector is positioned so you are not walking back and forth in front of it, casting your black shadow up on the screen. Nothing screams amateur presenter more than inadvertently playing shadow puppets in the middle of a PowerPoint® slide.

Make time to "meet and greet" your audience

Be in the room early. Shake hands and say "hello" to people as they come into your banquet hall or enter the conference room for the meeting. Putting names with faces and having brief but meaningful conversations with participants will set most speakers at ease. It helps you remember you are "among friends" and that your audience wants you to succeed. When a speaker flops, it makes everyone in the room feel uncomfortable. No one wants to feel uncomfortable, and no one wants you to fail or be bad.

Nothing screams amateur presenter more than inadvertently playing shadow puppets in the middle of a PowerPoint® slide.

Some of the most highly rated professional speakers I know will stand at the convention room door one hour early awaiting the first attendee's arrival. They shake hands, converse briefly with audience members as they enter, and even refer to some of them by name throughout their presentations. Personalizing the presentation thusly is yet another way to show the presentation is all about them, the audience, not you, the speaker.

✓ NO-PANIC Notes

"Dress and appearance are a crucial aspect of communicating who we are—our values, our self-image, our self-respect. Since about 90 percent of your body is covered with clothing, the way you dress is crucially important."

Bert Decker
You've Got to Be Believed to Be Heard

■ ■ ■

"What you wear makes a difference in what your listeners hear."

Doug Smart, CSP

■ ■ ■

"Yes, judgments about the worth of your words are influenced by the condition of your shoes."

Linda Edgecombe, CSP

■ ■ ■

"We quickly decide whether someone is worth listening to as they reach the podium."

Janice Hurley-Trailor

■ ■ ■

"You never get a second chance to make a first impression."

Old advertising slogan

Deal with Difficult Speaking Situations

CHAPTER D is designed to help presenters shine in seemingly impossible situations. The pages that follow provide proven techniques to help any presenter prepare for and successfully handle concerns, issues, and opportunities that may arise in a variety of speaking scenarios. For instance, what do you do if you have a hostile heckler in your audience? What if someone asks you a question you have no idea how to answer? We can group these troubleshooting opportunities into two categories: dealing with difficult conditions and dealing with difficult audience members.

Dealing with difficult conditions

Setting the stage for success is a first step to shining as a presenter and satisfying any early nay-sayers while at the same time avoiding any difficult meeting conditions. Industrial psychologists tell us as presenters we have three minutes to make a good first impression with a group. After that, everything you say and do will be seen and heard in the context of that first three minutes. This is a great truth. What are some actions you can take in the first three minutes of your meeting to set the stage for success?

- Start on time. Never be late.
- Be well prepared.
- Be well groomed.
- Have the room set up and ready.
- Speak to participants individually as they come in.
- Clearly communicate your objectives early.
- Start with something meaningful.

We all know there are people who come into a sales demonstration or a professional development session just looking for something to complain about. They are one reason sweating the small details of a business presentation plays a key role in its success. First impressions are important, and good first impressions often serve to quiet nay-sayers and not give them anything to complain about early in the meeting. Planning is a must. Getting to the room to set up before the first audience member arrives is helpful. You never still want to be setting up while your attendees are coming in. It looks unprofessional and sets the wrong tone for your meeting. The physical environment affects everyone's attitude and will have an impact on the interaction. Having everything in place gives you the opportunity to start strong. You have the ability to create the meeting conditions most suitable for your audience and message.

Chapter S: Set the Stage for Speaking Success provides logistical reminders for getting your next business presentation off to a successful start. "Having a place for everything and everything in its place" proactively prevents initial negativity and possible disruptions from audience members.

Dealing with difficult audience members

You'll want to turn problematic participants into productive ones. After all, we strive to shine in our roles as corporate trainers, sales presenters, and association leaders.

Inevitably some executive presenters may become anxious when dealing with adult audiences. Maybe you are afraid someone will ask a question you don't know how to answer. Maybe you think a know-it-all will challenge what you say from the platform. Maybe you're concerned no one in the room will speak up or participate in exercises. Possibly you'll become flustered if several cell phones start ringing—and audience members actually answer them and carry on conversations still in the room. It's inconsiderate, but it happens. The last thing we want is for a situation to get out of hand during a presentation just because we don't handle it in a positive manner as the facilitator.

So, just who are some of these common problematic participants who can make even pros slightly nervous? What are some of the disruptive elements that if not handled in a professional manner can turn into nightmares in the business meeting environment or even a college classroom?

- The electronically attached participant
- The tough questioner
- The know-it-all
- The napper
- The hostile heckler
- The meeting whiner
- The noisy neighbor
- The rambler

The electronically attached participant

How would you describe this participant, who is very much connected with the outside world during your meeting? Here are a few telltale signs:

- Lets cell phone ring
- Causes a commotion when leaving the room to take a call

- Shuffles through papers in briefcase or purse searching for the ringing phone
- Takes the call and carries on a conversation during your presentation
- Returns late from breaks
- Texts people and plays handheld games rather than participating
- "Tweets" comments to fellow audience members during your presentation

How do professional presenters handle the disruptions caused by this extremely connected audience member? Consider a few constructive responses for dealing with people who are too unnecessarily connected with the outside world during your meeting:

What To Do

- Start on time yourself. It sends the right message.
- When the participant's phone rings, joke by saying you were expecting a call at precisely 11:23 (insert the appropriate time).
- If they are consistently late coming back from breaks or lunch because they've been on the phone, consider closing the door of the meeting room to communicate ever so subtly the courtesy of punctuality.
- Or, if they are consistently late coming back from breaks or lunch because they've been on the phone, start with a high-energy activity so they'll recognize they've missed something by not returning on time.
- Offer to help them catch up on what they missed during one of the next breaks.
- Adapt one of these lighthearted remarks to produce a chuckle but make the point when a participant's cell phone rings:

    "I think that's for me."

    "Tell them to circle the block one more time; we're almost finished here."

What Not To Do

Never reprimand them on the spot.

You can acclimatize any of these tried-and-true techniques to your personal situation when handling people who cause a ruckus by allowing their phones and personal handheld devices to ring during your presentation.

Of course, presenters proactively can diffuse this type of behavior by discussing the meeting ground rules up front and even reminding people after they return from breaks. Covering housekeeping items at the onset of a business meeting doesn't have to be boring. These are some of the topics you'll want to address during this portion of your presentation, and remember, it shouldn't take long.

- Welcome them to the meeting, and quickly remind attendees of the title and purpose of your presentation to verify they are in the correct location. Flight attendants humorously take the same approach as passengers board for a flight: "If Charlotte, North Carolina, is not in your travel plans today, you'll want to deplane now."
- Thank the audience up front for their promptness and attention.
- Review safety information such as the location of exits, location of fire extinguishers, what to do if the fire alarm sounds, safe locations in case of a tornado (believe me, it happens), and what to do in case of a health emergency such as a heart attack.
- Preview the agenda and time schedule of your presentation.
- If appropriate, point out break times and the lunch procedure if your presentation lasts all day.
- Explain the locations of restrooms, coffee, and refreshments, and where they can step outside to take cell phone calls.
- Review cell phone etiquette.
- Introduce yourself and explain your credentials.

Take a few minutes to script out how you will creatively address housekeeping items up front when it's appropriate for the types of presentations you conduct. Use the *Idea Journal* page in *Chapter J* to write out your ideas. Be sure to use your imagination, and have fun with it.

We've described the characteristics of the electronically attached participant and discussed options for handling their disruptions. Now let's unpack solutions for dealing with the tough questioner. How do you handle it when someone asks a question you don't know how to answer?

The tough questioner

Tough questioners may:

- Ask a question you don't know how to answer
- Ask a question that is not relevant to the topic you're discussing
- Ask a question you just don't want to answer
- State objections to what you're saying in the form of a question

What are some ways you as a professional presenter can respond when you are asked a question you don't know how to answer—or simply don't want to answer?

What To Do

- Tell the truth. "I don't know how to answer that, but I'll find the answer for you when you return from break."
- Write the question on a sticky note, and post it on the questions board. Remember to clear your questions board before the end of the day if you use one. This is a general wall area, poster, or board to which audience members can affix a question throughout a long meeting or professional development class.
- Farm the question out to the audience. Say, "Let's see if anyone in the audience has an answer for that or has experienced something similar." Let the audience answer it for you.
- To buy a little time as you formulate your thoughts, restate the question or restate what you heard slightly differently. This helps those in the audience who didn't hear the original question, it gives you more time to think of an answer, and it provides the questioner a chance to clarify the question if you misunderstood it. The answer will come. Don't panic.
- Pause. Walk back to the lectern and look at your notes. The silence may be painful to you but not as noticeable to others.
- Keep your mouth closed and your mind focused as you formulate your answer; don't fill in the silence with "ummm" and "uhhhh" and other vocal fillers.

What Not To Do

- Never just make up an answer and lie, thinking they'll never know.
- Don't delay answering the question until the end of the session, and then conveniently "forget" to come back to it.
- Once you've responded, don't go back and say, "Does that answer your question?"
- Don't scowl and fold your arms across your chest in a closed mannerism; audience members will know the question has "thrown you for a loop," so to speak.

As we learned in *Chapter A: Analyze Your Audience*, professional presenters anticipate questions they might receive. So, as you plan your presentation, plan for questions, too. Write out questions you may be asked and practice answering them. Listen carefully to the question, and always repeat it or paraphrase it before responding. Keep your answer brief and simple, and answer with confidence and respect for the one who asked. Then, stop talking. Don't ramble. Respond specifically and move on to the next question or your closing clincher.

The know-it-all

We've talked about how to work with the tough questioner. Now let's move on to the next potentially difficult participant on our list: the know-it-all. How can we turn this possibly problematic participant into a productive contributor who doesn't get on everyone's nerves?

During my presenter orientation, the training managers shared various nicknames for the know-it-all class member: "show-off," "dominator," "motor-mouth," and "overly talkative participant." We speaker trainees were given these warning signs to be on the alert for a know-it-all in the room:

- Likes to be the center of attention
- Has an opinion on every topic and wants the audience to hear it
- Always has one better example, otherwise known as the "That-Ain't-Nothin'" complex

- Attempts to gain control, power, and attention by talking and sharing opinions
- Consumes valuable meeting time, even the extra cushion time you've built in

What To Do

Here are a few techniques for getting know-it-alls to open their minds and shut their mouths:

- Give them a special job to do
- Use their name often
- As the presenter, physically move away from them or withdraw your eye contact
- Remind all attendees there may be several different points of view in the room
- If you can tell their comments are getting on others' nerves, you can use some of these buffer phrases:

  "Let's get some input from others."

  "That's one point of view. Are there others?"

  "Who else has something to add?"

  "Thank you for sharing that example. Does anyone else want to comment?"

These responses take some practice, so do rehearse them out loud so they will be on the tip of your tongue when the time is right.

Reduce the negative influence of a conversation hog by having a system in place for discussions you facilitate:

  Pass an audience microphone for permission to speak

  Throw a soft ball around the room to share ideas

  Have them write their responses before sharing them out loud

  Use a timer

What Not To Do

Don't tell them to "shut up!"

The napper

Let's deal with an embarrassing meeting participant: the napper. Have you ever had someone fall asleep during one of your presentations? What do you do if there's a snoozer in the room?

Your goal with the person who chooses your meeting for a siesta is simply to wake them up and regain their attention without getting egg on their face. Below are some techniques I've used personally when dealing with those participants who occasionally fall asleep during one of my seminars. Yes, I admit it: it happens. I've had people snooze during my seminars—and it's hard not to take personally!

Yes, I admit it. I've had people snooze during my seminars— and it's hard not to take personally!

What To Do

- First, don't embarrass the person, and ascertain the problem is not a medical one
- Plan high-participation activities to support your main points
- Use plenty of interactive techniques to appeal to everyone in the room
- Avoid long lectures
- Don't turn off the lights for slideshows
- Check the lighting in the room beforehand; you may wish to bring in extra lamps
- Keep your own passion and energy level high

What Not To Do

- Don't embarrass them awake
- Don't point them out to everyone else
- Don't have everyone tiptoe out of the room, turn off the lights, and leave them alone
- Don't say "Boo!"

The hostile heckler

Our next difficult meeting participant is described as the heckler. Teachers in classrooms recognize this behavior quite quickly. You know it instantly when you have someone displaying this behavior during your presentation:

- Is a wisecracker
- Is very vocal and will let the entire room know if he or she is not happy
- Makes remarks that are inappropriate and borderline offensive
- Gains pleasure from challenging and confronting other participants and even the presenter
- Sometimes says rude comments you may not be aware of outside of the presentation room during breaks
- Can be heard saying something along the lines of, "I have better things to do than wasting my time here in this meeting"

What To Do

What would you do if you were presiding over a meeting of 20 people, and one of them was very obviously a heckler? Provided are a few constructive approaches:

- Remind them of any courtesy ground rules you established during housekeeping announcements.
- Then, you may have to approach the individual and say something such as this after an offensive remark: "I'm sorry; I didn't hear you. Did you have a question?"
- Let the other participants confront them. Usually the audience can take care of the problem for you.
- Talk to the person privately.
- Perhaps allow the audience member to air out his or her concerns.

Sometimes addressing the problem directly is a better approach. Consider these responses when speaking privately with a heckler:

- "I hear what you are saying; it has been my experience that...."
- "That sounded like a jab; was that your intent?" This is a great line from professional speaker and conflict management expert Marilyn Sherman of Las Vegas, Nevada. She finds hecklers most often will back off after that direct approach.
- "What would you do differently?" "How would you handle this?" Ask questions to involve them.

What Not To Do

- Never blow up and argue back.
- Avoid becoming negative with the heckler. It damages your credibility with the rest of your audience.
- Avoid using the word "but." The word "but" cancels out anything positive that precedes it. "That's a good idea, BUT...." "I understand where you're coming from, BUT...." And don't replace "but" with "however." "That's a good idea, HOWEVER...." As we discuss in my grammar and usage seminars, "however" is just a BIG BUT.

The meeting whiner

How can we turn this complaining participant into a productive contributor who doesn't drive everyone in the room banana bread? We're talking about the constantly complaining participant. How do you know you have a whiner in your meeting?

- Searches for things to complain about
- Makes negative comments
- Can be heard saying:

    "They made me come, and I didn't want to."

    "I can't do this."

    "I don't know why everyone else seems to like this?"

Here are some constructive techniques for communicating with meeting whiners and complainers during your meeting:

- Call them by name often
- For group activities, put complainers with several positive participants who want to be there
- Involve them in some special way
- Don't take the whines and complaints personally
- Remain in control
- Perhaps have a private talk with the constant complainer
- Limit any negative person's time to comment so you reduce their contagious negativity

- Allow them to get their frustrations out, and then respond one of three ways:

    Listen and then simply ask to move along

    Listen and deal with the problem instantly

    Listen and promise to deal with it later or at the end

What Not To Do

Don't respond with obvious irritation. Showing frustration reflects your lack of ability to handle the situation and reduces your credibility in front of the group.

The noisy neighbor

This is your class clown or your friendly neighborhood chatterer. The noisy neighbor:

- Likes to have a good time
- Volunteers to go to any seminar, meeting, or training session available
- Figures it's better to be at a meeting than at work
- Is not as interested in what you have to say as much as taking advantage of a day away from the office to play—at your expense
- Talks a lot during the meeting
- Engages in private conversations that can be bothersome to nearby attendees and, of course, the presenter

What To Do

You can adapt the following techniques to your next event when dealing with these chatty and sometimes disruptive audience members:

- Deal with them gracefully. Perhaps approach the people having the side conversation and just stand by them. This is what I do in my seminars if necessary.
- Simply walk toward them and present your material closer to them. That's one good reason for having a remote to forward your slides.
- Gently touch their chair, desk, or table and ask if they have a question. Some resources recommend you touch them on the shoulder

lightly, but I don't believe that's a good idea. I don't recommend touching someone without permission.

- Allow for longer meeting breaks, or set up a designated time to provide for social interaction.
- Let them know privately at a break that you and others are finding their conversations and interruptions a problem.
- Use your own body language. Stop talking and give them direct eye contact.

What Not To Do

- Don't ignore the behavior and hope no one else notices.
- Don't ask them to share their comments with the entire group. That's what my high school teachers always did!

The rambler

Finally there's the rambler. This is the meeting participant who wants to talk just as much as the presenter. This audience member goes on and on and on.

What To Do

- As the lead presenter and facilitator, jump in. Say, "Thank you for sharing," and call on someone else.
- Break eye contact with the rambler.
- Call attention to the time and agenda to refocus.
- Consider stepping in when the rambling participant comes up for air.
- Move the discussion along with a question for someone else.
- Summarize what was said and move along.

If the rambler interrupts another audience member, say: "Let's hear the rest of what Lawrence has to share."

What Not To Do

Whatever you do, don't hand over your personal microphone to a talkative audience member. You instantly lose control of your agenda—and you may never get your microphone back.

Bonus: **D**

<u>D</u>ress for a Successful Presentation

THESE ARE SOME of the most common questions about dress I am asked in my classes:

> *"What does 'business casual' really mean?"*

> *"What do you, the presenter, wear if the meeting is 'business casual'?"*

> *"How do you know if you're dressed appropriately for your sales presentation?"*

Below is a bulleted list of dressing do's and don'ts. Read them, and then decide which ones are appropriate for you to follow. A great starting point is to ask: "What does my audience *expect* me to wear?"

- When in doubt, dress one level "up" from your audience. For example, if they are wearing khaki pants and golf shirts, you'll look out of place and uncomfortable in a buttoned-down three-piece suit and power tie. That's two or three levels up from your audience. In this scenario, consider wearing a dress shirt with no tie or maybe just a blazer or jacket over your golf shirt. Women, pantsuits would be appropriate here.
- Avoid busy patterns and multicolored suits. Solids look better and often more professional from the platform.
- Wear darker colors when speaking in front of large audiences. Surprisingly, this helps them see you better.
- Press your clothes.
- XYZ: eXamine Your Zipper.
- Remember to remove your nametag before you speak.
- Check a mirror immediately prior to your talk.

- Follow the *1 + 1 Rule* for men's and women's suits: 1 primary color + 1 accent color. Men, your accent color typically is your tie, or it could be your dress shirt. Women, your accent color may come from your scarf, your blouse or shell, the trim of your suit, or maybe even a piece of tasteful jewelry.
- Apply minimal cologne or perfume.
- Remove gum or candy from your mouth before you enter the room.
- Check your teeth in the mirror as well. Watch out for that unwanted pepper flake or speck of parsley left over from lunch.

OUCH! Lesson Learned the Hard Way

One day I spoke to a group with a throat lozenge in my mouth. One evaluation revealed that an attendee "couldn't believe I would get up there and eat candy while speaking." I guess I should have told them it was a cough drop. Nonetheless, think about how distracting it is when you're listening to someone talk with a piece of hard candy stuck in her cheek or clicking against her teeth. The point was well taken.

Above all else, wear clothing colors that flatter your complexion and coloring, and choose styles that complement your body type.

Image expert Janice Hurley-Trailor of Scottsdale, Arizona, offers this overriding advice for men and women presenters: "Strive to look current and attractive: As human beings we are naturally drawn toward those two traits when first meeting someone, particularly seeing someone on stage."

Women

- Ladies, leave the distracting jewelry, heavy makeup, loud perfume, and "big" hair at home.
- Avoid the "too little" tendency: too little makeup, too little jewelry, too little skirt, too little clothing—seriously. Business presentations are not the ideal time to be "bringing sexy back."

- Stay away from your favorite animal print blouse, bright floral jacket, and even pronounced hound's tooth patterns. Those are distracting. They don't look good from the stage, and they don't look good on camera. Plus, they can make the folks on the front row a tad dizzy!

- Measure your skirt length. When up on stage, you'll want your skirt length to fall anywhere between one inch below the knee to one inch above, depending on your body type.

- Heed the three-piece-of-jewelry rule in addition to your wedding band and watch. Remember dangling earrings and jingling bracelets can be annoying and distracting to your audience.

- Stick with closed-toe shoes. No one wants to look at your toenails while you are talking.

- Yes, get that manicure. Keep your nails clean, short, and polished with a neutral color. A great excuse to go to the salon!

- Be careful not to walk into the meeting with your sunglasses atop your head.

OUCH! Lesson Learned the Hard Way

While still on the five-cities-in-five-days seminar circuit several years ago, I traveled and taught business writing seminars. My firm provided overhead transparency projectors for writing examples for audience members to see. After a class in California, I was gathering my evaluations once all the participants had left, and I noticed one of them included a personal message: "Mandi, you may want to rethink your jewelry. Your charm bracelet clinked on the glass every time you wrote on the projector and was quite annoying." I had collected charms for that treasured bracelet for years, yet I knew I could no longer wear it while speaking.

Remember, nothing dates you more quickly than your hairstyle. Keep your cut and color current and fresh. Have an honest friend assess your hairstyle.

Janice Hurley-Trailor concurs: "Many times we hold on to a hairstyle and clothes that were from our 'best days'—you know, when you were 30 and looked fabulous. Those same clothes and certainly that hairstyle should change as you do. Looking out of date will give the impression that your message is also out of date."

Men

- Men, button your coat.
- Polish your shoes, front and back. As Andy Griffith's character attorney Ben Matlock recommends: "Pay attention to the backs of your shoes; that's the last thing people notice when you leave the room."
- Wear a light-colored dress shirt under your jacket; it shows up better and complements most facial tones.
- Understand the implications of suit color: black suits are perceived as very formal; brown suits strike more of a relational vibe (think President Ronald Reagan wearing warm brown suits in the debates and when addressing the American public); and navy and gray suits exude a confident, professional air.
- Make sure your nails are trimmed and clean.
- Wear ties that reflect your personality without going overboard. I recommend conservative ties with a splash of red or a bright color to my executive speaking clients.

Great guideline: Pay attention to how the decision makers of the organization dress, and use that information to guide your wardrobe decisions.

Now what?

- Ask questions about audience attire proactively.
- Whatever you wear, make sure it reflects your personality—tastefully, of course. Perhaps all of this wardrobe and appearance advice can be summed up best in the words of image expert and success coach Janice Hurley-Trailor: "Highlight the best, and forget the rest."
- Always check the mirror before a presentation.

> Make real eye contact with individuals in your audience
> as if you're talking one on one with each person
> for three to five seconds.

"The face is the mirror of the mind, and the eyes without
speaking confess the secrets of the heart."

Saint Jerome

■ ■ ■

"The eyes trump the ears."

Connie Dieken

Engage the Eyes

LET'S DISPEL these two myths for presenters who are nervous about direct eye contact:

Myth One: Focusing on a spot on the back wall directly above people's heads will make it easier and will look natural.

Myth Two: Staring at a spot on someone's forehead gives the illusion of direct eye contact.

No and no. Make *natural* eye contact. After all, how do you feel when someone is talking with you but not looking you in the eyes? Are you suspicious? Are you wondering if you can trust them, if they're being truthful, or if they're hiding information from you?

The solution for what we call natural eye contact is to speak individually *to* your audience members, not *at* them. How believable are you when you stand up and say, "Good morning. It's great to be here today," while you're looking down at your notes or staring at the floor in front of your feet? They won't even believe your "Good morning."

Instead, make real eye contact with individuals in your audience as if you're talking one on one with each person for three to five seconds. It helps to divide the room into quadrants and alternate your focus to avoid favoring one side of the room (a common tendency among amateur facilitators). For instance, you pinpoint someone in quadrant one and talk to that person for three to five seconds. Then you move your attention to someone in quadrant two and talk to that person for three to five seconds. Then pick someone in quadrant three followed by an individual in quadrant four. Focus on different meeting members in each quadrant every time. Mix up the routine by changing the one-two-three-four pattern. Sometimes look at someone in quadrant three, then move to quadrant one, then back to quadrant three, then over to quadrant four. This is what we call in the world of professional speaking "how to work a room." The people sitting in the back feel just as much a part of the discussion as the folks sitting up front. Participants on the peripheries are not forgotten or ignored. When there's one "happy face" in the room paying attention, nodding in agreement, and laughing wholeheart-

When there's one "happy face" in the room paying attention and laughing wholeheartedly at your jokes, be aware of your inclination to focus mostly on that person.

edly at your jokes, be aware of your inclination to focus mostly on that person. After all, he or she is giving you the positive feedback you're longing for, so it's all too easy to direct most of your attention to that person. The same can be said for the gruff-looking or bored-looking participant seated in the back of the room with his arms folded across his chest. You may be so eager to win that hard-nosed attendee over to your side, or at least get a smile out of him, that you direct all your energy toward him at the risk of alienating others in the room.

OUCH! Lesson Learned the Hard Way

When I worked on the public seminar circuit, we would have surprise auditors. One showed up unannounced at a seminar I was conducting in San Antonio, Texas. (You always knew an auditor when you saw one: They would walk in three minutes before starting time and sit on the front row with a big clipboard and checklist in hand. I'm sweating just thinking about it again!)

At the end of the program, the auditor and I debriefed. He said, "Mandi, do you realize you spent at least 90 percent of your time standing on the left-hand side of the stage talking to that side of the room? You very rarely even glanced at those of us seated on the right. I'll bet if we check your evaluations, those on the right rated you lower than people seated on the left."

He was correct. Ouch! That's when I put the quadrant technique into practice.

A few other poor eye contact habits professional presenters need to be aware of include:

- Talking to the screen

    No one wants to look at the back of your head all day because you are reading your presentation from the same projector screen they are viewing; plus, most of the time they can read it for themselves.

- Reading from your laptop at your stage table

    You'll be accused of looking down too much. Again, don't talk to your visuals; talk to your audience.

- Staring at your lectern notes too long

- Having rapid eye movement

    Scanning back and forth across the people in the audience rapidly does not constitute natural eye contact.

- Staring at the same person in the same spot in the room

- Focusing only on the decision maker

  This happens in sales presentations when the decision to buy is made by a committee, but there's one chief executive in the room everybody is trying to impress. You unknowingly may convey to the others in the room their opinion is not as important when the only eye contact you make is with the business leader. People do notice. I can remember being in class several years ago with 14 in attendance and one VIP. We were seated in a horseshoe configuration, and the teacher made constant eye contact with the VIP every week. They were friends, and I'm sure he had no idea he was doing it. In fact, I figured I was the only one who picked up on this teacher's habit, but others in the room noticed it as well. The undue excessive focus had to make his friend feel a bit uncomfortable because it looked as if he were speaking only to him.

Practice making natural eye contact in your daily one-on-one conversations with people also.

Now what?

Realize we do tend to gravitate toward certain sides of the room and even certain sides of a conference table when making seated presentations. You may tend to talk to and make eye contact with people on one side of the table more so than the other.

Your homework is to begin practicing the quadrant technique the next time you're up in front of a group. That way, you make the people in the back feel just as much a part of the presentation as people nearer to the front. Both sides feel equally involved as well.

Bonus: E

Energize Your Environment

EVERY THREE MINUTES in a business presentation of any type, you want to have at least one element of your talk appeal to the visual, auditory, and kinesthetic learners in your audience. This is called the *Three-Minute First Impression* rule, and seasoned speakers take it very seriously. You run the risk of losing your audience and missing out on new business or receiving low speaking evaluations if you ignore the *Three-Minute First Impression*. And it's not limited to just the first three minutes—it's every three minutes.

It's not limited to just the first three minutes—it's every three minutes.

What are you doing every three minutes into a presentation to keep it fresh and interesting? Sometimes we fall into the trap of just dumping information on our audiences. Sometimes we use the excuse that our material doesn't lend itself to demonstrations or participation. That's when we have to get creative.

The following list offers very simple ideas to keep everyone in your audience alert and involved. It's up to you to incorporate one of these ideas (or one of your own) at least every three minutes into one of your sessions or speeches.

The best time to use these ideas is when you *get stuck*. Sometimes you're just not feeling creative. Sometimes you've been asked at the last minute to pull together an executive presentation. Fall back on this list to help you.

Some items are suited for small sales presentations with only two or three in attendance; some are geared more for the corporate trainer who conducts workshops. It's up to you to pick and choose the techniques that fit with your personality and style and that will be well received by your audience.

Energize your environment by incorporating some of these simple interactives:

- Demonstrate a procedure with the help of a participant
- Every three minutes, ask an open-ended question of an audience member
- Show a short video—*short* being the key word
- Provide literature, magazines, newspapers, and samples for participants to review, especially during sales presentations; hand them out at the proper time though because you probably don't want people flipping through your materials before you even have a chance to start
- Use a prop
- Pass the prop or sample around the room so participants can "touch and feel" it
- When there is a good reason, have participants change seats and tables; it changes their perspective just by switching locations
- Ask true/false questions spontaneously, and present a prize to the volunteer who answers and explains correctly
- Switch PowerPoint® slides at least once every three minutes
- Simply ask participants to raise their hands to answer yes/no questions
- Change your location in the room; e.g., go stand in the rear of the room when explaining a new idea so audience members have to shift in their seats to see you
- Break meeting attendees into partners for simple pair-and-share questions
- Ask someone in the audience to share a personal example to support the subject
- Use an analogy to paint a word picture
- Share startling statistics to show the relevance of the subject—no boring stats allowed

Energizing your meeting environment also means you do what you can as the presenter to appeal to your attendees' five senses. Consider playing music as people enter the meeting room. Having music in the background stimulates conversation among meeting attendees as they enter the room; moreover, it can feel a little awkward to the early arrivers to walk into a silent room, dull even. Having several conversations already in progress fills the room with energy as others enter. Very few people want to come in and just sit in silence. Music sets the mood. Just make sure the music you play is in the public domain. You don't want to be found guilty of violating certain copyright laws by playing popular protected music in a public meeting place.

Stimulate the sense of sight with a PowerPoint® montage running before the meeting starts. As appropriate, hang posters, set materials on the tables, and have a visually pleasing professional environment.

Serving food at any meeting almost ensures a good crowd shows up! I believe it is worth the added cost to have a simple breakfast and coffee for early morning meetings, a midday energy pick-me-up for those business meetings that fall around 10 a.m., and I wouldn't dream of holding a 2 p.m. meeting without snacks. Industrial psychologists even recommend salespeople avoid scheduling their presentations to buyers or decision makers between 2-3 p.m. Statistically speaking, you are less apt to make the sale at that time because for many

Serving food at any meeting almost ensures a good crowd shows up!

people it is the slump in the workday. Even job search specialists and headhunters encourage applicants to schedule their career interviews during the morning rather than afternoon. They call 2 p.m. the "death slot," not because of the candidate but because the interviewer may be tired and not fully attentive. Therefore, I personally arrange to have granola, yogurt, fruit, a variety of sweet treats, and mixed nuts along with water and sodas served to my audience any time I'm speaking to a group after lunch. It's still amazing to me how excited some grown adults get about a chocolate brownie in the afternoon! Other ideas to appeal to the sense of taste include having peppermints on the meeting tables and using assorted small chocolates as rewards for volunteers who answer questions or participate in any interactives.

The food in the room appeals to the sense of smell as well. Coffee percolating not only pleases the caffeine addicts, but it also creates a warm pleasant fragrance. There's something else you can do. What I'm about to share with you now is reason alone to be reading this book: The most valuable secret weapon in my briefcase is a travel-size Scentsy® room spray. Yes, I arrive at the presentation location before anyone else gets there and spray a light citrus scent in the four corners of the room. Doing so eliminates any mustiness, even foul odors, and freshens the room. I buy these in bulk and keep them in my car and the kitchen. I keep one packed in my suitcase to spray in my hotel room when traveling on the seminar circuit.

To appeal to the sense of touch, have props or samples set out for people to pick up and inspect. Always be ready with a warm handshake as they come in.

✓ NO-PANIC Notes

The video camera never lies.

F

Forget Fidgeting

HERE'S A PARTIAL LIST of "favorite fidgets" I've collected from **No-Panic Presentation Skills** participants:

- Twirling your hair
- Stroking your chin
- Clicking your pen cap
- Tapping the lectern
- Touching your note cards unnecessarily
- Playing with papers
- Pointing at people with your laser pointer
- Jingling coins in your pocket (called The Banker)
- Fiddling with your keys (called The Key Executive)
- Playing with rings and other jewelry (called The Jeweler)
- Constantly checking your watch
- Pacing with no purpose
- Messing continually with the microphone
- Touching or pulling on your clothing constantly

- Buttoning and unbuttoning your jacket
- Readjusting your tie
- Scratching your head
- Taking your eye glasses on and off
- Playing with your own props even when you're not referring to them

People notice. Some focus on the nervous habit so much they become distracted from the message. For example, some college fraternity members started a drinking game based on how many times a television talk show host flipped her hair while on camera. I understand they consumed quite a bit of adult beverage.

The cure to cutting out these distracting behaviors, these pesky presentation mosquitoes, is to *video tape* yourself at least once a quarter (painful, but necessary). Read below to learn the steps involved.

Now what?

I have been speaking professionally full time for 15 years, and I still video tape myself at least once a quarter. I can't stand it! But the video camera never lies. If you have some annoying tic or gesture, the camera will catch it. You will see it for yourself. It is a crucial part of your rehearsal. This is also one of the most painful self-improvement methods for any professional speaker. Here's what you do:

One week before a conference presentation, set up in surroundings similar to where you'll be speaking. Reserve a conference room if necessary. Invite coworkers and colleagues in so you will have an audience. Try to have at least four people watch you practice.

If that isn't possible, invite some friends over to your home, pop some popcorn, and explain you need a mock audience for taping purposes. In lieu of friends, just arrange some chairs in the room. Set pillows or stuffed animals in the chairs to practice making eye contact. It sounds silly, but this is how I practice a new presentation. I place Elmo®, Clifford the Big Red Dog®, Buzz Lightyear®, and assorted teddy bears in chairs around my living room to create my audience. I've noticed they give excellent eye contact!

Now, here's the key: Set the tape aside for 48 hours.

When you view it 48 hours later, you'll be looking at it with fresh eyes and a fresh mind. You're not as immediately familiar with everything you said and did.

> **I place Elmo®, Clifford the Big Red Dog®, Buzz Lightyear®, and assorted teddy bears in chairs around my living room to create my audience. I've noticed they give excellent eye contact!**

Watch the tape with the pause button and a notepad close at hand. Draw a line down the center of a legal pad to create two columns. Label one "What I Like" and the other "What Needs Improvement." Pause every time you need to make a note. Write down what you like about what you see. Also, make note of anything you see that surprises you and you don't like. Include distracting gestures and repeated fidgeting.

Draw a box in the upper right-hand corner. Use tally marks to count your "ums" and "uhs" and other vocal fillers such as lip smacks and tongue clicks.

As you can imagine, watching a tape of yourself can be very revealing. One speaker had 37 "ums" in the first three minutes. You don't realize how often you do it until you hear yourself speak.

"A picture is worth a thousand words."
Arthur Brisbane

■ ■ ■

"Listeners get meaning from more than your words."
David G. Lewis

■ ■ ■

"Research on the effectiveness of spoken communication and how a message is perceived by the audience reveals **55 percent** of the message is perceived from body language and facial expression, **38 percent** is perceived from voice tone and paralinguistics, and only **7 percent** is perceived from the words spoken."
Paraphrased communication study conducted by
Dr. Albert Mehrabian, Professor Emeritus of Psychology, UCLA

■ ■ ■

"Effective communication is a total body experience."
Kafi Matimiloju

Gesture with Grace and Purpose

In **Chapter F: Forget Fidgeting**, we listed what *not* to do with your hands. So, what *should* we be doing with our hands during a presentation? Clients ask me all the time about steepling and pointing and other authoritative gestures. What do they really mean, and how does our audience perceive them? Quite frankly, I think steepling just looks corny and unnatural, and I would never recommend pointing to anyone or anything during a presentation. Even flight attendants refrain from pointing during the safety announcements. Notice how they use the two-fingered technique when locating the emergency exit path lighting and the exit rows. They know what we all know: Pointing can be considered rude. Yet, one of the most commonplace careless speaking habits I detect with my first-time executive speaking clients is the tendency to point at people while gesticulating.

We use purposeful gesturing to present a clearer and more dynamic message while projecting energy, enthusiasm, and confidence.

This is the first **No-Panic** speaking secret I reveal during my seminars: Our bodies whisper telltale messages to our audiences, and they can sabotage our credibility and authority with a group because people will believe our body language over our lip language every time. Our words and our body must be speaking the same language because if there is a disconnection between the two, our image and even our company's image can suffer. If you are speaking words of confidence but your body language doesn't exude confidence, it's a dead giveaway of an incongruent message. If you say "Good morning," but don't visually exude enthusiasm, then no one will believe your "Good morning." You're not convincing them it really *is* a good morning.

People will believe body language over lip language every time.

Think about it this way. Let's say you're a tad nervous before an upcoming presentation. Maybe it has been thrust upon you at the last minute, and you haven't had a chance to prepare as thoroughly as you wish. Maybe other urgent tasks demanding your immediate attention kept cropping up during your prep time, and suddenly you're 24 hours out, and you haven't even practiced. Or maybe you've sat in the audience of a speaker who was visibly unprepared for the presentation at hand. It was obvious through that presenter's body language he or she had not conducted a crucial audience analysis and had not practiced key components of the speech. The speaker was uncomfortable, and it showed. But how do you know? What are some of the visual body language cues that denote anxiety?

- Fidgeting
- Poor eye contact
- Flighty eyes
- Hands in pocket
- Spastic gesturing
- Looking at notes too frequently
- Sweating
- Splotchy complexion

These bad habits will show up on your video-taped rehearsal. You will want to replace them with graceful and purposeful gesturing. Below are some gestures with positive inferences along with some negative ones to avoid:

Gestures with positive implications
- Hands open and palms up
- Large meaningful gestures in your personal power zone
- Anything that naturally complements what you are describing
- Leaning forward

Gestures with possibly negative implications
- "The Fig Leaf"   Hands clasped demurely down low
- "Dishpan Hands"   Hands behind back
- "The Banker"   Hands jingling coins in pocket
- "The Key Executive"   Pointing keys at people
- "The Close-Minded Professor"   Crossed arms
- "Mothering"   Hands on hips
- "The Jeweler"   Fiddling with jewelry, twisting rings
- "The Timekeeper"   Constantly glancing at watch
- "White Knuckle Syndrome"   Gripping the lectern tightly
- Picking at clothing
- Pointing with index finger
- Hands in steepled position
- Gripping laser pointer or pen too tightly

While we're on the subject of nonverbal know-how, nothing breaks the ice like a smile. This falls under the heading of building instant rapport and credibility with the people to whom you speak. A simple smile is a key contributor to the likability factor. People do business with people they like. People vote for people they like. I know some people who are casual and fun loving in their daily lives, yet when it is time to take the stage, they suddenly take on some serious stone-faced presenter's persona. As we say in the South, all of a sudden, they look like they just swallowed a big jar of pickle juice. Be aware of your own facial expression when you are in a meeting. When you catch yourself frowning or tense, relax your face. Begin to be more conscious of this. If you don't do it for any other reason, follow Dolly Parton's advice, who in the movie **Steel Magnolias**, said: "Smile, Honey, it increases your face value!"

Reality: People are much more likely to pay attention to what we're *showing* them from the stage than what we are *saying* to them. Our words and our body language must be in sync. Gesturing should enhance—not distract from—the presentation. We should be using our hands for meaningful gestures that complement our spoken message.

Now what?

Remember these helpful hints during your next presentation:

- Gesture in your personal power zone. It's the length of your arm span, out in front of you and above your head. The gestures may feel "big" at first, but they will look natural to your audience. Any props you use and any samples you hold up should be in your personal power zone so everyone can see them.
- Refrain from pointing at your audience.
- Resist the temptation to stick your hands in your pockets or behind your back. Your audience may think you are hiding something from them or holding back some information.
- Don't forget to smile.

✓ NO-PANIC Notes

"The monuments of wit survive the monuments of power."
Sir Francis Bacon

■ ■ ■

"A smile is a crooked line that sets everything straight."
Phyllis Diller

■ ■ ■

"Laughter is the shortest distance between two people."
Victor Borge

■ ■ ■

"A happy heart is a good medicine and a cheerful mind works healing,
but a broken spirit dries up the bones."
Proverbs 17:22

■ ■ ■

"He that is of a merry heart hath a continual feast."
Proverbs 15:15

■ ■ ■

"The joyfulness of a man prolongs his days."
Ecclesiastes 30:22

■ ■ ■

"Smile, Honey, it increases your face value."
Dolly Parton in Steel Magnolias

Highlight with Humor

FOR YEARS, the same question was volleyed about the hallways and meeting rooms during conventions of the National Speakers Association: "Should you use humor in a presentation?" The rote response was: "Only if you want to get paid!"

You, too, effectively can use humor in your presentations—even if you don't think you're funny.

Audience members like speakers who use humor, and they tend to be more receptive to your message.

However, humor has its share of do's and don'ts:

DON'T start with a joke for the sake of starting with a joke. Instead, make sure it ties in with your message and is a logical fit for your audience. Avoid the old "a duck walks into a bar" routine.

DON'T overpromise, saying "This is the funniest joke you've ever heard."

DON'T bill yourself as a humorist unless you are; otherwise, they'll be expecting a stand-up comic.

DON'T even think about jokes that pertain to sex, religion, politics, race, age, disabilities—or one's hair color!

DON'T include off-color jokes, even if you know people will laugh.

DO poke fun at yourself, not audience members.

DO practice your joke at least 20 times out loud. If you don't, you risk "laying an egg" in front of your actual audience. At best, you'll get sympathy laughter. Jokes always sound better in your head.

DO use more one-liners. Longer jokes are less effective.

DO pause before the punch line. It's not as funny if it has to be repeated.

DO be prepared for your humor to bomb; those can be some of your funniest moments.

What do you do if your joke fails and you "lay an egg"? Recover professionally by tying it immediately to the point you are trying to make, as in, "The reason I shared this is...." Later, go back and revisit it. What failed? Was it your timing? Did you step on your punch line? Are you the only one who thinks it's funny? Should you try it one more time, or just drop it?

What if you're not a natural jokester? Good humor is not restricted to telling jokes. Humor and warmth can be found in personal stories, cartoons used with permission, quotations from others, PowerPoint® slides, funny comments your children say, or even a personal catch phrase you use throughout the presentation to reinforce a sticking point.

Your life has more funny material than any joke book. Find it. Be on the lookout for it. Recognize it, and be sure to capture it in your *Idea Journal.*

Now What?

Years ago I clipped this quotation out of a book and placed it in my humor file. Cliff Thomas's thoughts on humor are the ideal test for knowing if you should use a joke or humorous one-liner. Allow me to share these wise words from Dr. Terry Paulson's book *Making Humor Work,* Thomson, Boston, Massachusetts, 1989.

> *"When someone blushes with embarrassment...*
> *when someone carries away an ache...*
> *when something sacred is made to appear common...*
> *when someone's weakness provides the laughter...*
> *when profanity is required to make it funny...*
> *when a child is brought to tears...*
> *or when everyone can't join in the laughter...*
> *It's a poor joke!"*
>
> —Cliff Thomas

Use this as your litmus test for incorporating good meaningful humor.

"I hear, and I forget; I see, and I remember;
I do, and I understand."

Confucius

■ ■ ■

"Every person you meet knows something you don't.
Learn from them."

Unknown

■ ■ ■

"Our lives are shaped by the places we go,
the people we meet, and the books we read."

Charlie "Tremendous" Jones

I

Involve Your Audience

IN COMMUNICATION SKILLS 101 classes on college campuses across the continent, students learn an interesting statistic during the first week: People formulate their first impression of you within seven seconds of meeting you. It's true. Apparently we live in quite a judgmental society whereupon the first few seconds of meeting someone new, we think we have them all figured out based on the clothes they are wearing, what their hair happens to look like that day, and the sound of their voice when they speak. Fortunately for presenters, we're given the benefit of a bit more time before listeners decide they like us and want to hear more, or they don't really care for us and they've tuned us out. It's called the presenter's *Three-Minute First Impression*, and seasoned speakers take it very seriously. We're given more than the standard seven seconds; we're given a full 180 seconds to make a good impression on our audiences and the value they'll derive from what we share. There are actions you must achieve during that opening three minutes to connect with your target audience.

There's one people group in particular who witness the three-minute rule lived out very regularly: members of the clergy. Pastors in churches tell me they can look out at their audiences on any given day

It is important to create an environment appealing to the visual, auditory, and kinesthetic attendees.

of worship and quickly see who has tuned in to their message and is actively listening—and who in the congregation already has tuned them out and has begun passing notes and making plans for lunch. They say it is almost as if they can see individual light bulbs over the heads of people either turning on or clicking off within the first three minutes.

Likewise, as the presenter or facilitator, it is important you create an environment appealing to the visual, auditory, and kinesthetic attendees, be there five decision makers in your sales presentation or 50 students in your classroom. Gone are the days of "speakers lecture and listeners sit." Rather, people effectively receive information in three different styles.

Visual Learners
"Show Me"

- Simple lecture alone does not work
- They need to be able to "see" what you are talking about
- They respond and retain your information better when you present it visually
- They want to have your content in writing to take away and "look at" later
- They like props, visual aids, and prefer maps to spoken directions
- They use language such as "Do you *see* what I'm saying?" and "How does that *look* to you?"

Auditory Learners

"Tell Me"

- They focus on words and sounds
- They are engrossed in the written and spoken word
- They need to hear what the speaker and others in the room are saying
- They like the logical progression of ideas
- They don't always look at the presenter because they are mentally processing the information shared
- They listen for key words and phrases
- They use such language as "I *hear* you," or "Do you *hear* what I'm saying?" or "That *sounds* right to me"

Kinesthetic Learners

"Involve Me"

- They are described as physical or manipulative learners
- They learn by doing
- They learn most easily when you involve them in the content and allow them to participate
- They don't want just to sit there
- They don't want just to hear about activities or look at examples
- Their motto is "move more"
- They are going to retain and remember more vividly those main points in which they participate
- They are "hands-on" learners

What are you doing to hook your auditory, visual, and kinesthetic learners during your opening, during your first three minutes especially? Consider these possibilities. There's no need to restrict them to the first three minutes: Use them throughout the important message you're conveying to them. Try using one of these action ideas *every* three minutes.

Action Ideas for Visual Learners
"Show Me"

- Use colorful posters and decorations throughout the room and on the tables
- Be liberal with visual aids such as slideshows, charts, posters, props, short videos, and other multimedia
- Demonstrate specific techniques
- Use excellent eye contact
- Have them read aloud from their learning guides if there is a lot of written material
- Give them something to look at with every key point

Refer to a main point in your speech or a specific module of your presentation. List the tools and techniques you currently use or may incorporate to meet the needs of the visual learner. Here's an example from one of my presentations to use as a model.

Main point: The importance of nonverbal communication

Technique: Model the six bad habits we do with our hands while speaking

Technique: Have five volunteers come on stage for charades

Continue for each main point of your presentation. Refer to the ***Visual Planning Guide***.

The NO-PANIC PLAN *for Presenters*

 Visual Planning Guide

How Do I Keep My Visual Audience Members Involved?

❏ Main point to support: _____

_____

_____

_____

❏ Which aspect appeals to visual learners? _____

_____

_____

_____

❏ Do I need props for any interactives? _____

_____

_____

❏ How much time should I allot? _____

_____

_____

❏ What else could I try with this main point to appeal to visual audience
members? _____

_____

_____

Later notes: What worked well visually? _____

_____

_____

_____

_____

Action Ideas for Auditory Learners
"Tell Me"

- Tell a story
- Include opportunities for them to listen and then paraphrase
- Explain any visual aid; don't just give it to them
- Always include captions and labels with visuals and pictures: Every table needs a label, and every photo needs a caption or cutline
- Create smooth and natural transitions with your language, e.g., "Step #1, Step #2"
- Include descriptive narratives and support your main points with personal experiences as illustrations
- Choose your words carefully, painting vivid mental pictures for your auditory audience members

Refer to a main point in your speech or a specific module of your presentation. List the tools and techniques you currently use or may incorporate to meet the needs of the auditory learner. Here's an example from one of my presentations to use as a model.

Main point: The importance of being prepared to capture ideas for speeches

Technique: Tell my story about being stuck in traffic in Kansas City

Technique: Have them list four places they come up with their best ideas

Continue for each main point of your presentation. Refer to the ***Auditory Planning Guide***.

The NO-PANIC PLAN *for Presenters*

 Auditory Planning Guide

How Do I Keep My Auditory Audience Members Involved?

❑ Main point to support: _____

_____

_____

_____

❑ Which aspect appeals to auditory learners? _____

_____

_____

_____

❑ Do I need props for any interactives? _____

_____

_____

❑ How much time should I allot? _____

_____

_____

❑ What else could I try with this main point to appeal to auditory audience members? _____

_____

_____

Later notes: What worked well auditorily? _____

_____

_____

_____

_____

Action Ideas for Kinesthetic Learners
"Involve Me"

- Provide ample opportunities to get up and move
- Use *meaningful* games
- Involve them in role play

Refer to a main point in your speech or a specific module of your presentation. List the tools and techniques you currently use or may incorporate to meet the needs of the kinesthetic learner. Here's an example from one of my presentations to use as a model.

Main point: Audience members have certain rights and expectations

Technique: Have training teams move to flip charts stationed throughout the room to write and "flesh out" each right or participant expectation

Technique: Ask participants to act out or demonstrate what we've discussed

Continue for each main point of your presentation. Refer to the ***Kinesthetic Planning Guide***.

The NO-PANIC PLAN *for Presenters*

 ## Kinesthetic Planning Guide

How Do I Keep My Kinesthetic Audience Members Involved?

❏ Main point to support: _____

_____

_____

_____

❏ Which aspect appeals to kinesthetic learners? _____

_____

_____

_____

❏ Do I need props for any interactives? _____

_____

_____

❏ How much time should I allot? _____

_____

_____

❏ What else could I try with this main point to appeal to kinesthetic audience members? _____

_____

_____

Later notes: What worked well kinesthetically? _____

_____

_____

_____

_____

On the day of this writing, I just sat through five presentations on a community college campus where no one planned their opening remarks well. They just got up and started with the standard boring "Thank you for having us here," and "Good morning. It's good to be here today." Not one of them involved the decision makers in the crowd, nor did they capitalize on the presenter's *Three-Minute First Impression* rule. No one stood out from the other four, and they were all competing for the same business.

Now what?

Don't get stuck in a speaking rut! Open with one of these simple techniques to kick start your next business presentation.

ASK an open-ended question.

BEGIN with a series of questions where they can respond by raising their hands.

GET them laughing or smiling with you.

CONDUCT a pair-and-share exercise.

SIMPLY DO something to get them to nod in agreement or shake their heads in disagreement.

Whatever you choose, involve your audience early on in the process and set up a give-and-take environment. Few people want simply to sit and listen to a lecture anymore. They want to be a part of the presentation.

Bonus: **I**

Incorporate These Instructional Ideas

AS YOU PRESENT NEW IDEAS, consider incorporating one of these methods as a fresh approach to mix it up. We were taught these techniques during the two-week orientation for new seminar leaders and even were tested on them, so they are ingrained in my mind. They have proven invaluable in my career of teaching adults. I've used almost all of these.

Consider a *case study*, whereby you present your case to your audience. Break them into teams of three to five, and have them analyze the situation and present recommendations.

Use a *demonstration* to involve others in the business meeting. You can do this even in one-on-one sales presentations. My husband is a master of this. He travels throughout four states selling sporting goods. Sometimes he is presenting to a sales team of 12; sometimes it is just he and the store owner. Regardless, he has his potential buyers try on and break in the baseball gloves, personally handle the new technology in footballs and basketballs, and even try on some of the new sublimated team jerseys. He shines the spotlight on their input, reactions, and ideas.

Have audience members participate in a meaningful and relevant exercise—not just a game for the sake of having an interactive.

Play a *game*. Have audience members participate in a meaningful and relevant exercise—not just a game for the sake of having an interactive. And again, this is not just for those readers who are corporate trainers and classroom teachers. You can use this approach in an informational business meeting or even a sales presentation. Bob will use sports trivia questions at the beginning of his presentation. His buyers don't think of it as "playing a game;" it's simply an innovative way to get them involved and interested in what he is about to tell and show them.

Plan an *interview*. Take it one step further by having participants interview another SME (subject matter expert) besides you. Even interview audience members as a planned part of your presentation.

Engage the group in a *next-seat neighbor discussion*. Generate participation by asking attendees to discuss an issue with their next-seat neighbor, stimulating questions and answers. As the facilitator, don't allow a few participants to go off target and start "chasing rabbits."

Don't allow boredom to breed. Invite other experts to participate in a *panel discussion*. Consider facilitating a planned conversation on a selected topic with two or three other experts; this is especially helpful when presenting different points of view on your topic or attempting to achieve buy-in from different perspectives on a new companywide change or mandate.

Include *role play* as a presentation technique. Have audience members enact a situation, giving feedback.

Facilitate a *strength-and-weakness session*. Have audience members assess the strengths and weaknesses of a topic and then make suggestions. Suddenly, they've made your presentation for you, and remember, people do like to hear themselves talk.

Think about which of the above or other original idea you can use to turn your next lecture into a presentation that involves your audience instead of being one sided.

Now what?

Don't allow boredom to breed. Use this ***Interactive Planning Guide*** to spot check sections of your presentation to verify elements that appeal to your visual, auditory, and kinesthetic audience members.

The NO-PANIC PLAN *for Presenters*

 Interactive Planning Guide

Use this planning guide as an aid in organizing your interactives, exercises, openers, closings, discussion starters, group activities, and demonstrations.

❏ Title: _____

❏ Goal of activity: _____

_____

❏ Materials needed: _____

_____

_____

_____

_____

❏ Time allotment: _____

❏ Instructions: _____

_____

_____

1.

2.

3.

4.

5.

Which element appeals to:

❏ Visual learners? _____

❏ Auditory learners? _____

❏ Kinesthetic learners? _____

"The dullest pencil is better than the sharpest memory."
Unknown

■ ■ ■

"Don't let the funny stuff get away."
Jeanne Robertson, CSP, CPAE

Journal Your Ideas

I KEEP AN ***Idea Journal*** for each of my five main topics. That way I'm never at a loss for fresh material. Always get permission from others to share their stories. When quoting from articles, always give credit where credit is due.

OUCH! Lesson Learned the Hard Way

Remember to document the source and date in the margin of newspaper, magazine, and book clippings. I haven't always followed through on this, and now I have folders filled with scraps of paper I've cut and torn from publications—and I have no idea where they came from.

Industrial psychologists tell us we don't always come up with our best ideas at work seated at our desks or even staring at our computer screen. Think about it: Where are you and what are you doing when you encounter a fresh idea or innovative approach to a project you're working on. Indeed, sometimes we are in the least opportune locations doing the most mundane of tasks when struck with sudden bursts of brilliance: bathing, sleeping, commuting, exercising.

This is more than just nice-to-know information. For five years, my husband and I lived in a small apartment in Overland Park, Kansas. I was driving home from work one Friday afternoon only to find myself stuck in standstill traffic on loop I-435, notorious for snarls and jams during rush hour. We had invited some friends over to grill out, and I was beginning to sweat making it home before our guests arrived. This was in a long-ago and far-away era before the ubiquitous cell phone, so I had no way of calling them or even my husband to let them know I would be late. To top things off, I had yet to make the dessert—and no self-respecting Southerner would serve a store-bought dessert to company. What to do? At the time, the Kansas City area was home to a well-known pastry institution called Tippin's Pie Pantry. Tippin's offered several dozen varieties of pies every day, and I knew I was slowly approaching the exit where one was located right off the interstate. As soon as I could, I exited, ran into the pie pantry, and purchased a strawberry-rhubarb pie, their specialty. I hopped back in my car and made my way back into traffic.

Indeed, sometimes we are in the least opportune locations doing the most mundane of tasks when struck with sudden bursts of brilliance.

This was on a Friday. The following Tuesday I would be auditioning for a seminar company to travel and teach their technical writing class, and I had been working so hard on the material I would use for the audition. I had only seven minutes in front of a hiring committee, and I knew

I had to wow them from the very start. The *Three-Minute First Impression* was crucial for this presentation, yet I had the most severe case of writer's block. I was completely stymied for the opening. What could I do to really capture their interest on the subject of technical writing and keep them engaged in it for seven minutes? I just couldn't formulate a decent opening in my head.

Suddenly, stuck in traffic on I-435, it hit me: the exact wording, pauses, everything. It just clicked and flowed so well. You know how you word something in your mind and you think, "That's it! That's exactly what I want to say." Yet, you know you can't trust yourself to remember it even three seconds later? I had no choice: I had to ditch the pie into the backseat floor board so I could grab the Tippin's carry-out bag and write out my opening lines before I lost them. I have saved that paper sack for all of these years because it accounted for my largest speaking contract to date. It is a tangible reminder of how important it is to be prepared to capture our best and brightest ideas. These days, of course, we can use technology to accomplish the same. There are dictation apps and voice memos on our personal handheld devices. At the very least, I've been known to call my own voicemail and leave a message of the exact wording so I can remember what I said while hearing how it really sounds with the pauses and inflections.

We must be prepared to capture these ideas when they come to us. Idea journals are great collection plates for random thoughts and new ideas for presentations.

Here are some samples of what I'll collect and add to my idea journal or idea files:
- Related articles from newspapers and magazines
- Blog reports on specific subject matter
- Quotations
- Real-world examples from coworkers
- Funny stories I hear
- Funny stories that happen to me

- Funny stories that happen to family members
- Funny comments my own children say
- Expressions heard from parents or grandparents
- Brainstorms
- Illustrations
- Great one-liners from movies
- Song lyrics that apply to the topic
- Historical notes
- Ideas for exercises
- Sample visual aids

Now what?

That's it. Start an idea journal. Write down your ideas immediately. As the unknown philosopher admonishes, "The dullest pencil is better than the sharpest memory." I have included an **Idea Journal** page here to jump start your efforts. Use it to begin crafting creative approaches for your upcoming business presentations.

And remember, you shouldn't clip a cartoon, show a movie scene, play a popular song, use music, or quote someone else's lengthy story without express permission or even paying royalty fees. When in doubt about using work that's not original, DON'T.

The NO-PANIC PLAN *for Presenters*
✓ Idea Journal

"Let your energy and enthusiasm for your topic show."
Cheryl Stock

■ ■ ■

"The exact words you use are far less important than the energy, intensity, and conviction with which you use them."
Jules Rose

Know Yourself

Prepare *Yourself* physically, mentally, and emotionally before you speak. As we used to say in the seminar business, let's bring our "A Game" to the presentation today. My training managers shared these preparation tips and bits of advice during our intense two-week orientation before we "hit the road" on the seminar circuit. I've been following their advice for more than 15 years, and I pass along a few additional helpful preparation hints gleaned from years of learning the hard way. The better prepared you are, the easier it is to truly be yourself when you stand to speak.

Knowing yourself uplifts your presentation to a place of authenticity both mentally and emotionally. It means you do more than simply share facts with your audience, but you are able to open up with your own insights and experiences and stories. It means you don't have to come across as some smooth-talking almost mechanical robot who never misspeaks or struggles to find the correct word. People can smell a phony a mile away; they can tell if you are simply saying what you need to say to succeed at that given moment. Being yourself means rather than speaking *at* your audience, you come across as having a real conversation *with* them. They shouldn't feel as if they just sat through a polished speech.

Now what?

In a physical sense, here are some action ideas to follow in the days and hours leading up to your next business presentation so you can bring your "A Game" to the platform when it really counts.

Days Leading up to the Presentation

- Get a roster of the people who will be attending. Becoming familiar with their names and titles will enable you to relate better; moreover, you'll seem as if you are "among friends."
- Memorize your opening three minutes of your material so you can take advantage of the *Three-Minute First Impression*.
- Anticipate questions attendees may ask about any subject matter you are covering. Prepare your answers. Be ready to respond to any questions; better yet, address them up front in your presentation before they even arise. That's really bringing your "A Game."
- Rehearse. Rehearse. Rehearse.
- Video tape yourself as detailed in **Chapter F: Forget Fidgeting.** It's painful but necessary. The video camera never lies.
- Run through your slides prior to your meeting.
- Once on site, check out the meeting room, and set it up in advance if possible. You won't have to rush around the morning of the presentation moving chairs, tables, equipment, and breaking a sweat.
- Test every piece of equipment: microphone, computer, projector, DVD player, lighting, volume levels, etc.
- Walk every inch of the meeting room, checking for feedback from room speakers, items you could trip on, etc.
- Review your notes once—and only once. Don't stay up all night cramming. Use the time to color code your notes and put cheat notes everywhere.
- Just say "no" to alcohol the night before.
- Go to bed early, and get a good night's sleep.

Just Before Your Presentation

- Stretch and jog up and down the hallway or run the stairs. Get rid of excess nervous energy while loosening up your muscles.
- Drink room-temperature water with lemon to moisten your mouth and throat. Iced water constricts the vocal cords.
- Avoid consuming dairy products beforehand as they can contribute to throat congestion.
- Eat a light breakfast or lunch, but don't overdo it. Beware of the breakfast buffet; step away from the triple stack!
- In fact, eat a banana. They are considered nature's perfect food. After personally witnessing several high profile speakers backstage at conventions of the National Speakers Association quickly unpeel and eat a banana before being called on stage to present, I finally asked why they and so many other performers chose a banana. The answer: Bananas contain a calming chemical; plus they don't get stuck in your teeth. Who knew?

Beware of the breakfast buffet; step away from the triple stack!

- Loosen your vocal cords and get rid of any "frogs" by talking out loud.
- Wear comfortable clothing and shoes. It's not the time to break in a new pair of dress shoes.
- Double check the room setup one last time.
- Take one last look in the mirror.
- Meet and greet audience members as they arrive.
- Breathe.
- Remember: People are watching you, even before you start. Please make efforts to smile, not frown. No one wants to see the presenter apparently nervous or worried before speaking. They want to witness a good presentation.

Bringing your "A Game" to your next executive presentation or professional development session means you are prepared to make stand-up presentations, lead groups, and facilitate discussions. These preparation tips ready you for delivering a spot-on message with confidence, comfort, and control.

Lectern:
The piece of furniture a speaker stands behind

Podium:
The platform upon which the speaker stands

Lose the Lectern

YOU DON'T WANT A BARRIER standing between you and your audience. They won't feel as close a connection with you. Instead of blocking your body by standing behind the lectern, turn it to a slight 45-degree angle and stand to the side of it. That way you are in full view of your audience, and you still can peek nonchalantly at your notes if you need them.

Don't get tripped up on the difference between the lectern and the podium. Many speakers incorrectly refer to the lectern as the podium. So, here's our vocabulary tip of the day:

    Lectern: The piece of furniture a speaker stands behind

    Podium: The platform upon which the speaker stands

When working with audio-visual experts and with meeting room set-up crews, you'll want to be sure to use the proper terminology. After all, you may get some funny looks if you ask them to move the podium to the left side of the room; I don't think they'll be in favor of moving the entire stage.

In certain sales situations, removing the barrier of a lectern can be the little "mosquito" that separates you from the competition. For instance, if you and three other firms are presenting for an opportunity to do business with a prospective client, and if the other three speakers enter the presentation room and automatically set up behind the lectern, the fact that you move it to the side and don't use it reinforces your confidence in your product or service and differentiates you from the rest.

Occasionally, I have the privilege of working with pageant contestants in preparing them for the interviewing portion of the competition. I recommend they stand to the side of the lectern rather than behind it so they are in full view of the panel of judges, thereby demonstrating they don't need the crutch of a lectern or large piece of furniture to stand behind to answer any of the questions thrown at them. Again, it's a subtle nonverbal cue that conveys confidence.

Now what?

Easy idea: Turn the lectern to a slight angle and stand to the side of it instead of behind it. And if you don't need it, don't use it. I never speak from behind a lectern; I usually just push it to the corner of the stage and use it to hide door prizes, visual aids—and my purse!

While you're at it, check the area for any other barriers between you and your audience. Relocate any tables, rows of chairs, and even large plants that partially obscure you from the people to whom you're presenting.

✓ NO-PANIC Notes

> Start strong. End stronger.
> Memorize your first and last sentences.

"If it ain't on the page, then it ain't on the stage!"
Zig Ziglar

M

Memorize Your First and Last Sentences

THE BEGINNING OF YOUR SPEECH is no time for weak small talk and gibberish or "Good morning, ladies and gentlemen." That's what everyone else says, so set yourself apart from the rest. You still can be personable and welcoming without reciting a litany of those people you are welcoming to the presentation or boring them with fluff in the opening. We live in a somewhat cynical society where time is valuable and people don't tolerate what they consider a waste of time. More of our business-savvy audiences take a Sgt. Joe Friday attitude of "Just the facts, Ma'am; just the facts." Our audiences want us to wow them at the beginning and get to the meat of the message. They have people to see, places to go, things to do.

Nor is the beginning of your speech the time to tell people the joke you just heard out in the hallway two minutes ago. If you haven't prepared to say it, resist the temptation to ad lib. Instead, when you have a strong opening sentence you've practiced and prepared and can speak with confidence no matter the circumstances, you'll immediately tame the butterflies in your stomach and win your audience's attention. Start strong; end stronger. Memorize your first and last sentences.

Please don't hear me saying you should memorize your entire speech or presentation. Don't do that. Inevitably, you'll forget something, and you'll be standing there with that "deer-in-the-headlights-of-an-on-coming-car" look of fear. Audience members will know you've lost your train of thought or forgotten what to say next. There's absolutely nothing wrong with using notes or a teleprompter during your conference to stay on target and avert forgetfulness. However, you don't want to give the impression you need notes during your opening. You should be able to stand with confidence and deliver your opening remarks with great audience eye contact. Truly, you would be surprised at how few executive speakers attend to this important detail and actually spend the extra time memorizing their opening statements. You also would be surprised to realize how a strong beginning will set you head and shoulders above the rest of the crowd, especially if you are one in a series of speakers. For instance, in a sales presentation situation, all things being equal, how you start will be most memorable. The Law of Primacy and Recency reminds us people remember best what they hear first and last. First and last are critical locations in any speech.

A strong beginning will set you head and shoulders above the rest of the crowd, especially if you are one in a series of speakers.

When you are working on your opening remarks, first ascertain elements that appeal to your audience's visual, auditory, and kinesthetic learners. Remember the guidelines for making the most out of your *Three-Minute First Impression*. Then, you'll want to consider these three opening aspects *in order* as a thorough preview:

1. Attention-grabbing device or hook
2. Purpose for the presentation clearly laid out
3. Reason for listening/audience benefits

Attention-grabbing device or hook
- Tell a great opening story with which the audience can relate
- Ask a provocative rhetorical question
- Ask an open-ended question—and expect answers
- Share some startling statistics—no boring ones allowed
- Use humor, though not necessarily a joke
- Quote someone interesting
- Read the newspaper and tie in a newsworthy current event
- Involve them in a pair-and-share exercise or other immediate relevant activity off of which you can build your message
- BLUF your audience; give them the Bottom Line Up Front
- Begin with a series of "How many of you have ever...?" questions where they can respond by raising their hands
- Involve someone in a demonstration
- Simply do something to get them to nod in agreement or shake their heads in disbelief
- Open with a meaningful visual aid

Which of the above approaches can you use to get more creative with the opening of your next presentation?

Purpose for the presentation clearly laid out
Again, there are two categories of business presentations: action presentations and information presentations. This is where you clearly explain which one is the purpose of your speech along with your goal for the audience.

If it is an action presentation, let them know up front what you want them to do or how you want them to act differently.

If it is an informational presentation, preview clearly what you want them to know or understand better. Think in terms of your lead sentence. Share the *who, what, when, where, why,* and *how* about your topic, and remember to conclude by tying back to your lead sentence.

Reason for listening/audience benefits

Use benefit-laden language to explain:

> *"At the end of our time together, you will be equipped with two techniques for cutting your writing time in half, and you will have practiced each one, thus freeing up more time to focus on high-value activities."*

> *"I promise you'll walk away with at least one sure-fire technique for increasing your family's income by spending about six hours a month working from home—and doing what you love."*

Chapter T: Tell Them What You're Going To Tell Them delves into much deeper detail for each of these opening elements and provides several examples, but for now, assess your presentation's opening by using this checklist of quick-and-easy do's and don'ts.

DO use positive language

DO focus on the audience with "you" language, not "I" language

DO compliment the audience

DO show appreciation to the specific people who made your presentation possible

DO tell them how glad you are to be their presenter

DON'T simply repeat the presentation title

DON'T begin with the standard "Good morning, ladies and gentlemen and distinguished guests"

DON'T complain about the room setup, poorly working microphone, or any other meeting details

DON'T tell an unrelated or poorly delivered joke

DON'T say, "I'm really not as prepared for this as I would like to be"

Way Before You Open Your Mouth

When you think about it, your opening truly begins before you launch into your attention-grabbing, relevance-relating first three minutes. It begins with your speaker introduction. Your speaker introduction, usually presented by the conference planner, event organizer, or chief executive, sets the mood for your actual presentation. The speaker introduction should establish your credentials and explain why you are the ideal speaker for that group at that time. It should be short. Sometimes the speaker introduction rivals the length of the actual speech. It shouldn't simply be a restatement of your resumé; rather, it is a speaker-designed intro customized for each different audience.

Keep it short. Sometimes the speaker introduction rivals the length of the actual speech.

There's more to it than just handing your introducer your bio sheet and hoping they pick and choose the right items to share. There's more to it than having them read through your resumé. The introducer shouldn't be the one who has to dig for the facts and come up with what to say; instead, you, the speaker, are responsible for your speaker introduction. It is our job as speakers to make it easy for those charged with introducing us before a conference or meeting.

At a recent meeting of the Mississippi Society of Association Executives, the chapter president sat next to me at lunch and confessed, "You know, I never know whether I'm supposed to read an introduction verbatim or paraphrase it so it doesn't look as if I'm reading it." That's a fairly common dilemma, so here are a few tips for avoiding any confusion with your speaker introduction:

- Write it as a narrative.
- Double space it for readability.
- Type it in at least 12-point font.
- Read it out loud yourself.

- Before you send it, time it. Try to keep it under a minute. Mine takes 53 seconds to read—and it still seems long some days.
- Send it to the introducer ahead of time so they can practice it.
- Bring a back-up copy with you to the meeting.
- Don't just hand them your bio sheet or resumé.
- Request they read the introduction exactly as you've written it. I've seen some introducers really butcher the speaker intro by ad-libbing or trying to present the information in a different order. Sometimes the introductions are so bad, it is hard for the actual speaker to recover.
- Finally, have fun with it. Share something quirky that gets a smile out of your audience and reveals a bit of your personal side.

Now what?

Below is an example of one of my speaker introductions. Again, I compose a different introduction for each unique audience. This is one from a recent professional development session I conducted for 100 nuclear engineers in North Carolina. You are welcome to use it as a model.

Meet Your Presenter

With more than 15 years of experience on the seminar circuit, CSP Mandi Stanley works primarily with business leaders who want to boost their professional image and with people who want to be better speakers and writers. She has traveled throughout North America entertaining and educating more than 40,000 seminar participants, totaling 4000 platform hours. Some of her recent clients include:

The Nuclear Energy Institute in Washington, where she presented three seminars

The United States Air Force

Kimberly-Clark's World Headquarters

Oconee Nuclear Station, where she has conducted eight writing classes

She has facilitated more than 75 corporate training and pro-fessional development classes for our organization in Char-lotte, Cincinnati, Plainfield, and Spartanburg. It all began with a specialized writing class she designed for our corpo-rate security inspectors five years ago.

Mandi is a professional member of the National Speakers Association, the leading organization for experts who speak professionally.

In 2003, she was designated a CSP, Certified Speaking Profes-sional. Fewer than 9 percent of all worldwide speakers have earned this designation, and Mandi is the first Mississippian in history to receive this honor through the NSA.

She's a summa cum laude graduate from Mississippi State University with concentrations in English, communication, and management, and a contributing author to four books. Audiences appreciate her platform enthusiasm, interactive style, and content-rich messages. She and her husband Bob live in Jackson with their seven-year-old and four-year-old sons, which now explains her frazzled expression and the dark bags under her eyes!

She's here today to help us get our written messages across with the results we want.

So roll up your sleeves, crack your knuckles, and get ready to do a lot of writing!

Please join me in welcoming—CSP Mandi Stanley.

Please use the following **Idea Journal** page to craft your own speaker introduction based on the bulleted guidelines above. Include resume-worthy information such as educational credentials and specific work experience. Consider one fun fact that's a bit off the wall and will pique listeners' curiosity. Close with the benefit of this presentation for this audience at this time. Remember, even your own intro should be all about your audience.

As a practice exercise, dissect my sample intro above to identify each of these distinct elements. Then have fun writing your own.

The NO-PANIC PLAN *for Presenters*
☑ Idea Journal

"No passion so effectually robs the mind of all its power and reasoning as fear."

Unknown

N

Nix Nervousness

VARIOUS ORGANIZATIONS publish books of lists each year, and most include the "Top Ten List of Fears and Phobias." Year after year, the fear of speaking in public tops the list. One recent survey revealed the top fears in this order:

1. Public speaking
2. Heights
3. Snakes and spiders

I pretty much count on public speaking being the top fear every year as I travel and conduct seminars. One year it wasn't—and it messed me up for an entire 12 months! Do you know what the number one fear was that year: fear of dentists. Obviously, I wasn't qualified to travel and teach **No-Panic Dentistry Skills**, so I was out of luck until the next year's publication.

It's no secret that many people do not like to have to stand up and speak in front of a group. The mere thought makes them break out in hives.

Still, I recognize many people in my audiences and reading this book are seasoned professional presenters who have no problem with it. Indeed, some people truly are gifted in that area, love to speak in front of groups, and actually thrive off of the energy they receive from their audience members. Still, even the pros know as soon as you take the stage, so to speak, and as soon as the spotlight is on you, the anticipation of that presentation will manifest itself physically in some form or fashion, no matter how many years' experience you have and no matter how much of a subject matter expert you are.

So, let me let you in on a simple presentation skills truth: Your body reveals telltale messages to your audiences, which possibly can sabotage your credibility with a group because people always will believe your body language over your lip language. If you are speaking words of confidence, but your body is not exuding that confidence nonverbally, it's a dead giveaway. Listeners detect an incongruency in your message, even though they can't quite pinpoint it. Your body and your lips must speak the same language, because if there is a disconnection between the two, your image, credibility, and authority could suffer slightly.

What can cause such a disconnection? First, lack of preparedness and anxiety do go hand in hand. From my experience, not being fully prepared is a root cause of a case of the nerves before speaking, but it's not always your fault.

Think about it this way: It's 9 a.m., and someone just drops a presentation in your lap at the last minute, saying, "I was supposed to speak at the chamber of commerce luncheon today about our new community outreach program, but I've had something urgent come up. I need you to go in my place. It will be a breeze. They just need you to talk for 20 minutes." Whaaaat?!

Or, maybe you've known about the presentation for a while, but other priorities kept popping up, and all of a sudden, you're 24 hours out, and you haven't even practiced it. Some would blame that on procrastination, but it happens all the time in the working world.

Better yet, let's say you're in the audience of a business presentation, and from where you're seated, you can tell the speaker is not as prepared as he or she should be. Perhaps that speaker hasn't done due diligence. Because of a lack of homework and audience analysis, they are the wrong speaker with the wrong message for the wrong group, and it's uncomfortably noticeable, not just for the speaker but for the audience as well. How do you know? How can you tell? What telltale signs of nervousness is the speaker's body obviously communicating?

Quick exercise: Prepare a list of nervous symptoms. Start with what happens to you prior to a presentation. Then, what are signs of anxiety you've observed before with other speakers? Being able to identify these manifestations of nervousness is a first step to overcoming them.

When I ask this same question in my *No-Panic Presentation Skills* seminars and then list the answers on the flip chart, here are some of the responses I inevitably hear:

- Quivering voice
- Shaky hands
- Trembling knees and legs
- Sweaty palms
- Dry mouth
- Shortness of breath
- Rapid breathing
- Knots in your stomach
- Nausea
- Lack of focus
- Forgetfulness
- Blotchy skin
- Rapid heartbeat
- High-pitched voice

- Talking too fast
- Ums and uhs
- Poor eye contact
- Monotone delivery
- Excessive perspiration
- Fidgeting in a variety of forms
- "Deer-in-the-headlights" expression
- Constant swallowing
- Hives

These can sabotage any presentation—especially the nausea.

People ask me all the time: "Mandi, do you still get nervous before you speak?" I have to answer that question honestly. For me, the answer is: "No, I don't get nervous; I get excited." What we have to understand is that it is the same energy. If it shows up as good energy, we desire that. Athletes call that adrenaline, and it helps them bring their "A Game" to a sports match or race. However, if it shows up as bad energy, the many negative symptoms above are the result. It's up to us to channel that energy and go from nervous to very natural. We want to turn that nervous energy into good adrenaline by identifying the symptoms, taking control of our surroundings, and focusing on the audience rather than ourselves. We can turn panic into poise.

Now what?

Tips for Turning Panic into Poise

You can combat anxiety both mentally and physically. First, here are some mental tips for calming your nerves.

Remind yourself it's all about your audience.

Yes, lack of preparedness is one cause of nervousness. Consider also that when we are genuinely nervous, another contributing factor is— and let this sink in—that we're too focused on ourselves. When you concentrate on being a service to your audience, be it one person with whom you are meeting, or 1,000 people in a crowded convention center ballroom, you take the focus off yourself and place it where it should be: your audience. Very rarely does anything good come from fixating on questions such as: What if *I* mess up? What will they think of *me*? I wonder if they'll like *me*? I wonder if they'll think *I'm good*? I wonder if they like *my* new suit? Should *I* have worn the blue one instead? Suddenly, there are a lot of "I's" and "me's" floating around in your head. Turn that "I" focus into a "you" focus, and

We can turn panic into poise.

it will help settle a case of the jitters. And yes, they *will* like you as a result. You are giving your audience a gift: the special message you've customized solely for them.

Remember, you are among friends.

What a great approach! Your audience typically is on your side, and they want you to succeed. When a speaker flops, it makes everyone in the room feel uncomfortable. No one wants to feel uncomfortable, and no one wants you to fail or be bad.

If possible, get to know your meeting attendees.

Be in the room early. Shake hands and say "hello" to people as they come into your banquet hall or enter the conference room for the meeting. Putting names with faces and having brief but meaningful conversations with participants will set most speakers at ease. As mentioned in **Chapter C: Create Confidence**, some of the most highly rated professional speakers I know will stand at the convention room door one hour early awaiting the first attendee's arrival. They shake hands, converse briefly with audience members as they enter, and even refer to some of them by name throughout their presentations. Personalizing the presentation thusly is yet another way to show the presentation is all about them, the audience, not you, the speaker.

Look confident—even when you're not.

These are nonverbal cues you can control to let your audience know you
believe in what you are saying and doing. Confidence begins in the eye
of the beholder. Professional speakers know these secrets to looking
confident, even when they're a complete basket case on the inside. So,
check the mirror before you go on stage, and remember:

- Stand up straight
- Smile
- Make natural eye contact
- Let go of anything you are holding that shows you have "the shakes"
- Be yourself
- Don't forget to breathe

Pinpoint the root cause.

What are you actually afraid of? Looking bad? Losing your place? A
specific critical audience member who is out to get you? Malfunction-
ing equipment? For most of these genuine concerns, there is a proac-
tive solution.

Memorize your first sentence.

Absolutely, beyond a shadow of a doubt, know the first words that will
come out of your mouth. This may be some of the most helpful advice in the book. Know your first sentence.

**Your projector may
blow a bulb—
and a very expensive
bulb at that.**

When it's time to begin your presentation,
say it exactly the way you've practiced it.
Anything can happen the day of a presentation to throw you for a loop. You can be
expecting six people and suddenly 20 show up. Or, just the opposite:
You were expecting a large turnout, and only a handful of people are
there at starting time.

Anything can and will happen. Your microphone may fail. Your projector may blow a bulb—and a very expensive bulb at that. In Portland,
Maine, the hotel caught on fire, and we had to evacuate and regroup

outside. No matter what happens, the show must go on, and if the meeting conditions are other than you expected, you still need to be prepared to start strong.

The beginning of your presentation is no time to ad lib. Nor is it the time for weak gibberish or fluffy small talk. Nor is it a good idea to share a joke with your audience you just heard outside in the hallway five minutes beforehand. If you haven't practiced saying it, don't. Material always sounds better in your head. Rely instead on the opening sentence you've practiced saying with great eye contact. Here's a promise to even the most nervous of speakers who absolutely dread facing a group of people: Once you've gotten that first sentence out of your mouth, it's smooth sailing from there. You'll almost feel as if a load has been lifted because the worst part is over; the rest of your presentation will be much easier. For many anxious speakers, getting started is the hardest part.

Know your first sentence. Be able to say it backward, forward, upside down, standing on your head with your eyes closed in pig latin.

Absolutely memorize your first sentence. Practice it out loud. Be able to say it backward, forward, upside down, standing on your head with your eyes closed in pig latin. Know your first sentence.

Be comfortable with being uncomfortable.

Amanda Box, owner of Amanda Box Communication, advises her public speaking students to "be comfortable with being a bit uncomfortable." Box says to expect it. Here's what she asks her students to do: "Create an uncomfortable scenario before you give your speech to see what it feels like firsthand. Get up in front of your next staff meeting and make an announcement. Notice how it feels as people are looking at you. It is often the fear of what might happen that can heighten nervousness, so expect to be a little uncomfortable, and it will impact you less."

Pray.

Before going on stage, I recite Psalm 19:14: "May the words of my mouth and the meditation of my heart be pleasing and acceptable to you, O Lord, my strength and my redeemer."

Finally, be Peter Brady.

As we learn from this legendary episode of the classic television series "The Brady Bunch," when all else fails, just imagine your audience in their underwear.

The above are some mental solutions to overcoming presentation nervousness. Below are some very practical doable physical stress reducers:

Run the stairs.

One day prior to a conference, I ran into a good friend and fellow speaker running up and down several flights of stairs in his freshly pressed suit, power tie, and newly shined shoes. "Joel, what in the world are you doing? Did you forget something in your room?" His reply was, "No, I do this before every speech; getting rid of this excess energy helps calm my nerves."

Engage in quick vigorous exercise.

You can run the stairs like Joel. You can jog around in the hallway. You can jump up and down back stage. Dispensing your excess energy through movement works well; just don't get too sweaty.

Breathe.

Don't forget to breathe. Take a few deep breaths, and relax your shoulders as you exhale to relieve tension and tightness there. Much of fear is energy that needs to be released, and breathing and stretching help with that.

Stay warm.

Industrial psychologists tell us that the body gets colder when you are nervous. Therefore, drink room temperature water sans the ice, and perhaps bring an extra jacket to wear prior to your presentation.

Hold the caffeine.

Coffee and colas serve to heighten anxiety, causing you to become tense and slowing the flow of oxygen to your brain. For what it's worth, caffeine is a natural diuretic—and that's all I'll say about that before a presentation.

Get a good night's sleep.

Don't take sleeping pills, and try not to look at your presentation notes after 6 p.m.

Stretch.

Do a few neck rolls. Stretch your body and loosen up.

Actually, why *is* it always so cold in hotel meeting rooms?

O

<u>O</u>wn the Room

OVERHEARD at a recent conference in Orlando: "I am freezing in here!" "Why is it always so chilly in hotel meeting rooms?" "Good grief, it's cold in here." "I'm going back to my room to get a jacket." "I'm so cold I can't concentrate."

Actually, why *is* it always so cold in meeting rooms? That's a good question—and one I don't know how to answer. What I can recommend, though, is that as soon as you enter your speaking arena, be it a ballroom, an auditorium, a hotel meeting room, or your office's conference room, you instantly should become territorial. Take charge of the temperature. For the 30 minutes or the three hours of your presentation, you own that room, and it's up to you to create as pleasant a listening experience as you can for your audience. That means you're not just in charge of your content, your visual aids, and your attendees' handouts; you are deemed responsible for the room temperature, the comfort of the seating arrangements, ease of viewing of the screen, and even how far down the hall the restrooms are! And while you probably have nothing to do with *any* of these factors, your audience will view you as in charge of every element of the meeting's success. Working closely with the meeting planner or conference coordinator, along with creating your own meeting success checklists, will go a long way toward creating a comfortable learning experience for all involved. You may be a five-star speaker with an expertly crafted message customized specifically for your audience, but they're not going to view you as favorably if they're sitting in hard chairs in a room cold enough for hanging meat.

You may be a five-star speaker, but they're not going to view you favorably if they're sitting in hard chairs in a room cold enough for hanging meat.

Uncomfortable people aren't as likely to buy what you're selling or respond in the way you are hoping.

Most of these setting recommendations pertain more to those of you who are subject matter experts speaking at conferences, or corporate instructors in a classroom, than those who make one-on-one sales presentations in a prospect's office. After all, you more than likely wouldn't seek permission from clients to come to their office the night before the presentation to check the lighting and chair comfort. You're prepared to present anytime, anywhere, regardless of your environment.

My husband is a walking example of this. He has met clients and presented his products to them not only in their sporting goods stores but also in a police department lobby, in an old newspaper printing shop, beside a swimming pool, and even in a hut. He's not in charge of the surroundings; he just has to do the best he can regardless of the setting.

And while I, too, have found myself teaching classes in such odd settings as a barn, an active bowling alley, and a movie theater that still had a floor full of stale popcorn and other sticky substances left from movie-goers the night before, I generally have the luxury of working with my meeting contacts to create an ideal setting for learning and comfort for those in attendance.

One of the decisions your trusted meeting planner can help you make is the room arrangement.

Room arrangement
Conference table setup
- Good for groups of 10-12
- Provides table space for drinks, refreshments, and note taking
- Facilitates small group discussions and interaction
- Usually good view of speaker and visuals

Round tables
- Also called banquet style or rounds
- Ideal for meals during the presentation
- Ideal for small group discussions
- Good for note taking

One negative to a round-table setup is that several participants automatically have their backs to the speaker and must rotate their chairs 180 degrees to view the presentation. Also, it can be a noisy arrangement when surrounded by chatty neighbors and fork-to-plate-clicking meal enjoyers. Work with the meeting planner to decide whether the rounds will seat six or eight people comfortably and whether chairs around the front half of each table should be moved so that no one's back is to the presenter.

U-shaped tables
- My favorite
- Also called horseshoe style
- Ideal for small group interaction and taking notes on a flat surface
- Good view of speaker and the screen
- Limited number of meeting participants; not suitable for large audiences

Auditorium style
- Also called theater style
- No tables; simply chairs lined in rows
- Accommodates large audiences
- Ideal for short presentations; not full-day classes

Auditorium style is not the most comfortable for attendees, and it's not recommended when people will take notes or have food and drink. When auditorium style is your only option, offset each row slightly so that attendees won't be staring into the back of someone else's head. Pretend you are an observer and spot check several chairs in different areas of the room. Is there enough aisle space to move in and out of the row without stepping on fellow participants' feet or handbags? Are the stacking chairs locked together, or is there space to move about?

Classroom style
- Good for note taking and laptop setup
- Good view of presenter and screen
- Works for large groups
- Usually two or three people per table

One disadvantage is that participants see only each others' backs and have to move their chairs to engage in any type of group discussion.

Chevron style
- Variation of classroom setup with a v-shaped table arrangement with a center aisle
- Better for audience interaction than the typical classroom style
- Still good for note taking, computer setup, and eating and drinking

Once the table arrangement has been decided, it's time to pull out the equipment checklist. What will you need? The **Meeting Equipment Checklist** provides some options.

The **NO-PANIC PLAN** *for Presenters*

 ## On-Site Checklist

These questions can be answered by the meeting planner by phone or
e-mail and then verified on site:

❑ Name of meeting room _____

❑ Size of meeting room _____

❑ Room arrangement preference:_____
    ❑ Conference table
    ❑ Round tables
    ❑ U-shaped setup
    ❑ Auditorium style
    ❑ Classroom style
    ❑ Chevron style
    ❑ Other _____

❑ Maximum room capacity _____

❑ Equipment already in room _____

❑ Equipment meeting facility will provide _____

❑ Equipment speaker will provide _____

❑ Are there windows in the room? ❑ Are there curtains or blinds?

❑ Is there a clock in the room?

❑ Can the presenter control the lighting? If not, what is the contact's name
and direct number? _____

❑ Can the presenter control the temperature setting? If not, what is the
contact's name and direct number?_____

❑ Is room located near the restrooms? Are there enough stalls? (You don't
want a gathering of 300 women to go on break with only two stalls in the
adjacent restroom!) Are the restrooms clean and maintained well?

❑ **Big question:** Is there any construction going on in the facility near the
meeting room?

❑ Other information _____

_____

The NO-PANIC PLAN *for Presenters*

 Meeting Equipment Checklist

- ❏ Laptop and presentation software
- ❏ LCD projector
- ❏ Remote control
- ❏ Screen **If possible, place the screen in the right corner of the room.**
- ❏ Television
- ❏ DVD player
- ❏ CD or music player
- ❏ Video camera
- ❏ Flip chart paper and stand
- ❏ Colored scented markers
- ❏ Blackboard or white board
- ❏ Laser pointer
- ❏ Risers
- ❏ Lectern
- ❏ Extra lighting
- ❏ Extension cord
- ❏ Three-pronged adapter
- ❏ Transparent tape, masking tape, duct tape
- ❏ Microphone: wireless lavaliere, handheld, or attached to lectern
- ❏ Display tables
- ❏ Head table
- ❏ Back-up batteries
- ❏ _____
- ❏ _____
- ❏ _____

Then, there is my *Five-Senses Checklist*. It's a mini list I use during my room walkthrough to make sure I have achieved everything I can to appeal to the visual, auditory, and kinesthetic learners in attendance.

Imagine being the meeting-goer for a moment. Imagine walking through the doorway to a meeting (and it could be your third such meeting of the day) and being greeted by upbeat music playing lightly, the warm fragrance of coffee and pastries, and a humorous slideshow montage rotating on the screen at the front of the room as people arrive. Already you sense this will be a better-than-average meeting.

As the old saying goes: "The mind can absorb only what the seat can endure."

Finally, there's this hodgepodge of miscellaneous notes and observances I've collected through the years. I tuck away these recommendations in my "don't-leave-these-details-to-chance" file:

- Reserve your audio-visual equipment well ahead of time.
- Request a note pad and writing utensil for each participant.
- Furnish a written introduction to the meeting head.
- Ask the meeting chairperson or emcee to remind people to silence their cell phones and other personal handheld devices.
- For classes, post a couple of signs in conspicuous places to remind people to silence these devices and to step out of the room if they need to take a call.
- In rooms where there are many chairs but only a few bodies, section off the back portions of the room so people sit close to one another toward the front of the room.
- Check noisy meeting room doors. If the back doors click loudly when they close, ask someone at the facility to duct tape the door latch so it closes silently. I travel with tape in my briefcase.
- Make sure the room temperature is around 68 to 70 degrees.
- Verify there's adequate lighting in the room for note taking.
- Decide if you want the window shades open or closed. What's happening outside can be very interesting; I've been upstaged by window washers, people on smoke breaks making faces through the windows at those of us "trapped" in the meeting, and even a flock of geese. Make sure open windows don't wash out the slideshow.

- Ensure any electrical cords are taped down.
- Request a pitcher of water and drinking glass for the head table.
- Double check that all equipment is working properly and the sound level is appropriate for the room size and number of people who will be filling it.

If you want to be invited back to speak, follow my mom's advice to "leave every place you go better than you found it." One of my clients in North Carolina actually hands a room-cleaning checklist to instructors in their conference center and requests they review and initial each of the items *after* their classes.

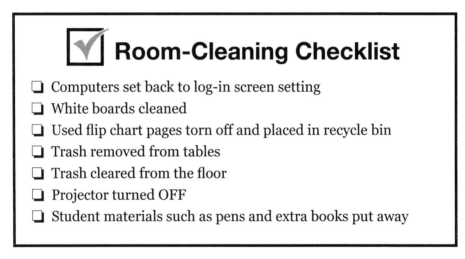

☑ Room-Cleaning Checklist

- ❏ Computers set back to log-in screen setting
- ❏ White boards cleaned
- ❏ Used flip chart pages torn off and placed in recycle bin
- ❏ Trash removed from tables
- ❏ Trash cleared from the floor
- ❏ Projector turned OFF
- ❏ Student materials such as pens and extra books put away

Now what?

While it may seem like overkill to some, attention to these details goes a long way toward creating a positive, memorable, and comfortable experience for those attending your meeting. As the old saying in education goes: "The mind can absorb only what the seat can endure." Audience comfort is crucial to their concentration.

Prepared speakers can "own" the room before, during, and even after their presentation.

The NO-PANIC PLAN *for Presenters*

Five-Senses Checklist

Sense of taste

Possible break-time items:

- ❑ Coffee (regular and decaffeinated)
- ❑ Hot tea/iced tea
- ❑ Variety of sodas (regular/diet)
- ❑ Water
- ❑ Fruit juices
- ❑ Pastries
- ❑ Bagels and cream cheese
- ❑ Fresh fruit
- ❑ Nuts and snack mix
- ❑ Chocolate candies, cookies, brownies

❑ Time of break? _____

❑ Length of break? _____

❑ Number to be served? _____

❑ Lunch menu? _____

❑ Dinner menu? _____

Sense of sight

- ❑ Room that is neat, clean, and orderly when people arrive
- ❑ Colorful posters and decorations throughout the room and on the tables
- ❑ Liberal use of visual aids such as slides, charts, posters, props, short videos, and other multimedia
- ❑ Something to look at with every key point

Sense of sound

- ❑ Music playing as people enter the room (music must be in the public domain)
- ❑ Conversations in progress to fill the room with energy
- ❑ No bleed-over noise from other offices or meeting rooms

Sense of touch

- ❑ Props and samples out and available for people to pick up and inspect
- ❑ Books already out on the tables

Sense of smell

- ❑ Pleasant smell of coffee percolating, food out and ready, etc.
- ❑ No noticeable unpleasant smells such as must or some foul odor

Oh, no, not again—I forgot my toothbrush.

P

Pack Your Bags

HAVE YOU REMEMBERED all the props and equipment necessary to make your presentation a smashing success? Provided are a few sample packing checklists. Use them to create your own.

This **Meeting Equipment Checklist** reflects the information in **Chapter O: Own the Room.** Here's how I use it. Typically by phone I review the list with the conference organizer or on-site contact to determine which equipment will be on hand at the meeting site and which equipment I need to bring with me. We simply run through the list together, and I check off what I need to remember as well as make special notes about who my audio-visual contact will be, how early we can meet to test the equipment, and the brand names of devices used to verify compatibility.

The NO-PANIC PLAN *for Presenters*

 Meeting Equipment Checklist

- ❏ Laptop and presentation software
- ❏ LCD projector
- ❏ Remote control
- ❏ Screen **If possible, place the screen in the right corner of the room.**
- ❏ Television
- ❏ DVD player
- ❏ CD or music player
- ❏ Video camera
- ❏ Flip chart paper and stand
- ❏ Colored scented markers
- ❏ Blackboard or white board
- ❏ Laser pointer
- ❏ Risers
- ❏ Lectern
- ❏ Extra lighting
- ❏ Extension cord
- ❏ Three-pronged adapter
- ❏ Transparent tape, masking tape, duct tape
- ❏ Microphone: wireless lavaliere, handheld, or attached to lectern
- ❏ Display tables
- ❏ Head table
- ❏ Back-up batteries
- ❏ _____
- ❏ _____
- ❏ _____

Once I've reviewed this information with the meeting professional, I then focus on my briefcase.

No matter how proficient and experienced you are, you *must* review your personal **Briefcase Checklist** before you head out to your meeting. A year ago, Bob was driving two and a half hours to Tuscaloosa for a sales presentation and to treat one of his good clients to lunch. He had less than half a tank of gas in his car and had planned to stop in Meridian to fill up. His fuel light popped on as he exited the interstate for the service station. He opened his console where he usually keeps his wallet and credit cards. No wallet. Unphased, he pulled out his briefcase and stuck his hand down in the front pocket to find it there. Not there either. Starting to sweat, he searched every pocket of his briefcase; then he moved to every nook and cranny of his other travel bags. No wallet, no money, no gas. Even if he could drive on fumes all the way to Tuscaloosa, he certainly didn't want his good customer to foot the bill for lunch. Finally, he called me to search all the possible locations at home to make sure it hadn't been lost or stolen, and I did find it—in the console of *my* car. What to do? Fortunately, I always tuck emergency supplies in the glove compartments of each of our vehicles, including an emergency $20 bill. That bill had been there for years, and we had forgotten about it. Was Bob happy to find that $20 that day! (He also found the emergency baby's diaper we kept stashed away.) He used $12 to get just enough gas in his tank to make it and had a few bills left for a drive-through burger and cup of water. His client accepted his rain check for lunch another time. That's reason enough right now to stop reading, go outside, and stick a $20 bill in your car for backup. Don't say you'll do it later; do it while you're thinking about it. Just avoid the temptation to pull it out to treat the family to ice cream when you're out and about. Forget it's there, for it truly is your emergency fund.

That's reason enough right now to stop reading, go outside, and stick a $20 bill in your car.

A **Travel Itinerary Checklist** and a **Suitcase Checklist** also will remind you to pack essential items.

The NO-PANIC PLAN *for Presenters*

 ## Briefcase Checklist

- ❏ Laptop and all cords and accessories such as the remote control and projector adapter
- ❏ Portable microphone and accessories including batteries
- ❏ Colored scented markers for flip charts
- ❏ Washable markers for white boards
- ❏ Back-up copy of presentation
- ❏ Extra master copy of any handout or learning guide
- ❏ Hard copy of the speaker introduction
- ❏ Legal CDs for music
- ❏ Extra power strip
- ❏ Props and visual aids for my program
- ❏ Cell phone and charger
- ❏ Reference materials
- ❏ Door prizes for presentation volunteers
- ❏ Candy
- ❏ Gift for meeting professional/event planner
- ❏ Blank thank-you note cards with envelopes and postage
- ❏ Writing utensils
- ❏ Wallet/billfold
- ❏ Airline tickets and other travel confirmation numbers
- ❏ _____
- ❏ _____
- ❏ _____

That's one big briefcase!

The NO-PANIC PLAN *for Presenters*

 Travel Itinerary Checklist

Make this checklist your one-stop shop for all things travel related. Consider creating one for each out-of-town presentation and storing it on your computer. This is one time I recommend redundancy and encourage printing the checklist to have a paper record.

❏ Airline _____

    ❏ E-ticket number _____

❏ Driver's license or other photo identification

❏ Hotel name, address, and phone number _____

_____

    ❏ Hotel confirmation number _____

    ❏ Room preferences:
        ❏ Suite
        ❏ King
        ❏ Double queen
        ❏ Nonsmoking
        ❏ Handicapped accessible
        ❏ Check-in time, check-out time _____

❏ Transportation arranged _____

_____

    ❏ Complimentary transportation to/from airport_____

    ❏ Phone number for taxi or town car _____

❏ Rental car company and phone number _____

_____

    ❏ Rental car reservation number _____

    ❏ Vehicle preferences _____

❏ _____

❏ _____

❏ _____

The NO-PANIC PLAN for Presenters

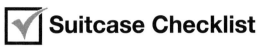 ## Suitcase Checklist

When packing your suitcase for a business trip, start at the bottom of your wardrobe and work your way up.

❏ Shoes
  - Make sure they are comfortable enough for on-your-feet presentations yet high quality to project a good image
  - Pack two pairs

❏ Socks or hosiery

❏ Your essential presentation wardrobe
  - Work several outfits out of one core suit to save room
  - Change the look with a different blouse and/or accessories
  - For men, pack different-colored dress shirts and ties
  - Choose travel-friendly fabrics such as lightweight wool
  - Don't forget your undergarments

❏ Accessories such as belts, jewelry, ties, and scarves

❏ Casual clothing for after hours

❏ Workout clothing and shoes

❏ Sleepwear and slippers

❏ Toiletries including makeup, shaving kit, toothbrush, etc.

❏ One set of emergency clothing for those unexpected occurrences and delays

❏ _____

❏ _____

❏ _____

❏ _____

❏ _____

❏ _____

OUCH! Lesson Learned the Hard Way

The first time I experienced a canceled flight for business was returning home from a presentation in San Antonio, Texas. For some reason, the airline evacuated us passengers from the plane but refused to remove our luggage. The plane ended up flying to our destination about four hours later, but we were stranded in San Antonio overnight—sans suitcases. San Antonio is a great spot in which to be stuck an extra night; there certainly are worse locations, but I had nothing: no toiletries, no clean clothing, no comfortable shoes, nothing to sleep in that night. The airline shuttled the passengers to the hotel, and I ended up buying some "I Love San Antonio" pajamas in the hotel gift shop. I've saved those pjs all these years as a vivid reminder of how important it is to pack some simple emergency clothing in my carry-on bag. It's a good thing, too, as I've been stranded in St. Louis; Albany; Dallas; and Madison, Wisconsin since.

Random Observations from 35,000 Feet

Finally here is a collection of eclectic observations pertaining to travel and presenting on the road.

- Oddly, I'm much more likely to forget something when speaking locally than when I have to fly to my presentation location. The lesson here is to use these checklists even if you're just hopping in your car and traveling 10 miles up the road for a presentation.
- At first, keep a list of items you forgot, and make sure you add them to the appropriate travel list. Some road warriors keep this list on their computer or personal handheld device; others keep the list in a side pocket of the luggage they use.
- Many women speakers I know have two makeup bags: one for home and one they keep in their suitcase at all times so they don't have to pack and unpack it every time they hit the road. Many men keep a separate bag of travel toiletries ready so they don't have to worry about leaving their razor or aftershave at home. I haven't quite attained that level of efficiency yet, but I'm working toward it.

- Suitcases marked with "Heavy" tags tend to be treated better and thrown around less by baggage handlers. Airlines do have weight limits on individual bags, usually 50 pounds.
- Airlines also require you to remove hanging straps and hooks from your luggage and store them in a side pocket, so save time by doing so before you leave for the airport.

Now what?

Create your own checklists for both local presentations and for those that involve travel. Use the ones provided as a guide.

✓ NO-PANIC Notes

"There is no evidence the tongue is connected to the brain."
The Tongue and Quill

■ ■ ■

"The human brain is a miraculous thing; it begins working the second you are born and doesn't stop—until you stand up to speak in public!"
Unknown

Quicken Your Wit

WHAT DO YOU DO if your projector blows a bulb in the middle of your presentation?

How do you respond when an audience member's cell phone rings?

What if your great opening story falls flat and all you hear are crickets chirping in the background where the laughter is supposed to be?

ANSWER: Have an arsenal of one-liners you have rehearsed but will appear spontaneous. The perception is that you're able to think—and speak—on your feet.

One must-have resource on this subject for any business speaker is *What to Say When You're Dying on the Platform: A Complete Resource for Speakers, Trainers, and Executives* by Lilly Walters, published by McGraw-Hill, Inc.

How you handle the unexpected reveals much about your professionalism. When conditions in your executive presentation environment are not as conducive to learning and good communication as you would like—or when something disruptive happens suddenly—your ability to respond in a lighthearted, even humorous, manner will enable you to remain in control while taking care of the problem. You'll get high marks for handling adversity with a sense of humor.

Remember, when faced with a fire alarm or a tornado alarm, it is no time to joke. Follow the appropriate evacuation procedure.

These are just some ideas to get you started. When I work one on one with video coaching clients, I hand them this homework sheet listing anything that possibly could go wrong during a presentation. I mostly use this with candidates for public office to be prepared for speaking at association luncheons, chambers of commerce events, Rotary Club meetings, and other stump speech scenarios. As much as it is an oxymoron, tucking away prepared one-liners for when these events occur while you are speaking will help you appear even more spontaneous. Your audience will never sense you've thought about these in advance.

What will you say when:
- The room is too hot
- The room is too cold
- The microphone acts up
- Your projector blows a bulb
- You hear a loud crash outside the meeting room
- You drop all your notes
- No one laughs at your joke
- You trip or fall
- An audience member's cell phone rings
- You forget what you were going to say

Now what?

Prepare some humorous remarks for each of these occurrences. The **Planning for Spontaneity Checklist** will get you started.

Hold a "comedy club" meeting with a few of your coworkers or friends to see who can come up with the best line. Then write them down and be prepared to use them the next time something unexpected happens during one of your meetings. I have provided the same homework sheet and checklist I give my clients for prep work.

The NO-PANIC PLAN *for Presenters*

 Planning for Spontaneity Checklist

Prepare both humorous and professional responses to these meeting scenarios so you will be able to think—and speak—on your feet when they occur.

❏ The room is too hot _____

_____

❏ The room is too cold _____

_____

❏ The microphone acts up _____

_____

❏ Your projector blows a bulb _____

_____

❏ You hear a loud crash outside the meeting room_____

_____

❏ You drop all of your notes_____

_____

❏ No one laughs at your joke _____

_____

❏ You trip or fall _____

_____

❏ An audience member's cell phone rings _____

_____

❏ You forget what you were going to say _____

_____

Remember, when faced with a fire alarm or a tornado alarm, it is no time to joke. Follow the appropriate evacuation procedure.

☑ NO-PANIC Notes

"Practice, practice, practice."
Orel Hershiser

■ ■ ■

"It usually takes me more than three weeks to
prepare a good impromptu speech."
Mark Twain

■ ■ ■

"By failing to prepare, you are preparing to fail."
Benjamin Franklin

■ ■ ■

"Quality is never an accident; it is always the result of intelligent effort."
John Ruskin

■ ■ ■

"I am the most spontaneous speaker in the world because every word,
every gesture, and every retort has been carefully rehearsed."
George Bernard Shaw

Rehearse. Rehearse. Rehearse.

BASKETBALL SENSATION and NBA Hall-of-Famer Michael Jordan has been quoted as saying:

> *"There is a right way and a wrong way to do things. You can practice shooting basketballs eight hours a day, but if your technique is wrong, then all you become is very good at shooting the wrong way. Get the fundamentals down, and the level of everything else you do will rise."*

What is worth doing is worth doing well.

For whatever reason, people have chosen to invest their time with us, be it 30 minutes, two hours, or a full day. We want to make sure their time spent with us is worth every last minute they've sacrificed to hear what we have to say. That means we care enough to practice.

Some speakers rather flippantly neglect practicing their presentations. Sometimes they deliver the same presentation 30 times a year and think they can forgo a quick run-through. Sometimes they are addressing the same audience every week with a different message and feel as if practicing out loud each week just isn't necessary. And, some business speakers are skilled enough to wing it, but simply put, your delivery just won't be as sharp without practicing out loud. A story may sound good in your head, but if you haven't practiced your wording and segues, it may fall flat with the audience. You may step on your punch line or fail to pause at just the right spot.

What aspects of our business presentations deserve practice?

Practice projecting PowerPoint® slides

- Practice enough so you know exactly where your slide transitions occur. Speakers with little experience tend to stop after a portion of their presentation, pause, turn to the screen, push the forward button on the remote control, wait for the next slide to appear, then turn around and start talking again. Slide transitions should be seamless; rehearse it in such a way that you don't have to turn around and look at the next slide to know what to say next.

- Know exactly where the projector is so that you don't walk back and forth between the projector and the screen, casting a giant shadow where the next slide should be. If the projector isn't attached to the ceiling, try to place it so that it's not awkward to walk all the way around it when moving to the other side of the room or conference table.

- Practice using a laser pointer to highlight information on the screen; every training manager I've had in my career has frowned upon using your hand or finger to point to something on the screen. The laser is more professional. In the same vein, watch out for the tendency to play shadow puppets as you gesture too close to the projector. Make friends with the magical "B" key; press it to blank out your screen when you don't need it.

- Obviously, don't talk to the screen—talk to your audience. Know your presentation well enough so you don't have to read it from the screen. As one business-savvy participant once commented: "If I had known I was going to be read to, I would have saved the time and asked the speaker to just e-mail me a copy the presentation."

- Make sure the people in your business audience see more than just your profile. Again, watch turning around too much and using the screen as your presentation prompter.

- In the same light, don't read from your computer. Many presenters take advantage of the "presenter's view" in many slideshow programs to sneak a peek at what comes next and even jot a few reminder notes. If you read from those notes too frequently, then all people will see is the top of your head. It's hard to make natural eye contact when you're looking down.

- Practice with the "pickle." Imagine my surprise when years ago, prior to the tragic events of September 11, 2001, I was conducting a run-through of my presentation with the audio-visual staff at the Marriott World Trade Center. Those folks were pros. I was scoping out the room, taking their suggestions for audio-visual placement, and doing a sound check as the next morning I would be addressing 300 professionals in the financial services industry. I overheard the a/v coordinator and an assistant asking where the pickle was and if I had tested the pickle for various blind spots on stage. What? Turns out, the pickle is the remote control—or at least audio-visual slang for it—and it is a good idea to determine ahead of time where you need to be standing to forward your slides. Many times there are spots in a room where the remote and computer can't communicate, and practicing with the "pickle" enables you to identify any dead spots before the real deal.

Practice with the "pickle."

Practicing with your slides is one area you don't want to leave to chance. Consider these other rehearsal methods prior to an important presentation—and they're *all* important.

- Practice out loud—always
- Repeat selected sections of your speech three or four times
- Rehearse in front of coworkers
- Rehearse in front of family members
- Invite some friends over, pop some popcorn, and let them be your audience
- Video tape your presentation

In ***Chapter F: Forget Fidgeting***, we introduced the process of video taping and then reviewing your presentation. Provided is the step-by-step process for one of the most painful self-improvement methods for any professional speaker:

1. One week before a conference presentation, set up in surroundings similar to where you'll be speaking. Reserve a conference room if necessary. Invite coworkers and colleagues in so you will have an audience. Try to have at least four people watch you practice.
2. If that isn't possible, invite some friends over to your home, pop some popcorn for them, and explain you need a mock audience for taping purposes.
3. If that doesn't work out, just arrange some chairs in the room. Set pillows or stuffed animals in the chairs to practice making eye contact. It sounds silly, but this is how I practice a new presentation. I place my children's stuffed animals and action heroes in chairs around my living room to create my audience. They make excellent eye contact—and they don't heckle!
4. Set the tape aside for 48 hours.
5. Watch it 48 hours later; you'll be looking at it with fresh eyes and a fresh mind. You're not as immediately familiar with everything you said and did. The 48-hour holding period is an important detail.
6. Watch the tape with the pause button and a notepad close at hand. Draw a line down the center of a legal pad to create two columns. Label one "What I Like" and the other "What Needs Improvement."
7. Pause every time you need to make a note. Write down what you liked about what you saw. Also, make note of anything you see that surprises you and that you don't like. Include distracting gestures and repeated fidgeting and words that don't sound quite right.
8. Draw a box in the upper right-hand corner. Use tally marks to count your "ums" and "uhs" and other vocal fillers such as lip smacks and tongue clicks.

As you can imagine, watching a tape of yourself can be very revealing. One speaker had 37 "ums" in the first three minutes. You don't realize how often you do it until you hear yourself speak.

Now what?

You can't master the fundamentals without practice. Choose at least one of the recommended techniques, and don't forsake practicing before your program. When you make practice a priority, as Michael "Air" Jordan confirms, the level of everything else you do will rise.

Speaker's stance is the sure-fire cure for purposeless pacing.

"A good stance and posture reflect a proper state of mind."
Morihei Ueshiba

S

Support Yourself with Speaker's Stance

CONTINUING WITH THE ANALOGY of the pesky "mosquitoes" that can creep into our presentations and distract members of our audience, we've already identified several: ill-prepared closings in **Chapter C**, inattention to dress in **Chapter D**, poor eye contact in **Chapter E**, fidgeting in **Chapter F**, unnatural gestures in **Chapter G**, mistakes in the presentation's opening in **Chapter M**, and nervous tendencies in **Chapter N**. Another small detail that can make a big difference in our delivery is a strong posture. That's where speaker's stance saves the day, and you don't even have to think about it too much.

To use my son's vernacular for a moment, speaker's stance is a "cool trick" we newbie speakers were taught during trainer orientation. Indeed, we were required to practice it every time we stood to speak, and our stance was scrutinized during the video-taping sessions. Why the emphasis on speaker's stance? Speaker's stance prevents lazy speaking habits such as:

- Crossing your ankles while speaking
- Locking your knees
- Resting all of your weight on one leg, aka the "Miss America pose"
- Slouching
- Rocking back and forth
- White-Knuckle Syndrome at the lectern
- Purposeless pacing at the front of the room

Speaker's stance looks natural and comfortable from your audience's perspective. It just takes a little practice to feel comfortable to you, too. Here's how it works:

Step One

Stand with your feet slightly under shoulders' width apart.

Starting with step one prevents looking stiff and rigid in toy-soldier fashion. Women, this still looks good even if you are wearing a dress or skirt, and it steers you away from the contrived "Miss America pose" where the heel of your right foot is positioned at a 45-degree angle into the side of your left foot, and most of your weight is resting on one leg. It appears too purposeful and overdone much akin to the "steepling" gesture some speakers practice.

Step one prevents looking stiff and rigid in toy-soldier fashion.

Step Two

Elongate your spine and assume good posture.

Imagine a string starting at your feet and continuing through your body all the way up to the top of the ceiling, pulling you into a straight and confident-looking posture. Step two prevents the bad habits of slouching in front of your business audience and draping your body over the lectern and holding on for dear life.

Step Three

Stand with your weight slightly forward in your stance, concentrated on the balls of your feet.

Experts tell us the balls of our feet are designed to support our body weight. Centering your weight on the balls of your feet eliminates another pesky presentation mosquito: rocking back and forth from heel to toe while talking. Have you ever noticed presenters who seem to start swaying and slightly swinging their arms while speaking? They are completely unaware they are doing it, so step three serves to secure their stance. Additionally, it is impossible to lock your legs when you focus your body weight on the balls of your feet. What happens when people stand up and lock their knees? They can pass out. Twice in my career I have witnessed this. The first time was on a university campus where the speaker was up on the platform in front of more than a thousand collegians; she unknowingly locked her legs and fell off the back of the stage. The good news is she was not hurt, but it can happen to anyone.

I would pace back and forth from one side of the room to the other. It was so bad I could actually spot my tracks in the carpet in some hotel meeting rooms.

Step Four

Let your arms rest naturally at your sides.

Many times we wonder what to do with these objects hanging from the ends of our arms, so we end up doing some funky things with our hands: pointing, playing with the remote, clicking a pen top, fiddling with our jewelry, crossing our arms, or even repeating the same movement again and again. Resting our arms at our sides frees us to do what we are supposed to do with our hands: use them for meaningful gestures that complement what we are saying.

One added benefit of speaker's stance is the elimination of purposeless pacing. Some presentation guides nickname this "wearing a rut in the stage." This used to be my worst habit. I would pace back and forth from one side of the room to the other for no apparent reason whatsoever; it was so bad I could actually spot my tracks in the carpet in some hotel meeting rooms. Can you imagine how annoying that was to the meeting participants? I'm sure the folks on the front row experienced mild whiplash. What a bad habit! I'm thankful someone shared this mental reminder with me: The only time you should walk from one side of the stage to the other is when you are figuratively indenting. What a great concept! It taught me to stand still while making a point and then casually change locations when it is time to tell a new story or move on to a new idea.

Now what?

It's your turn. Practice speaker's stance. Get comfortable with it. This is one time I actually do recommend getting in front of a full-length mirror so you can feel and see speaker's stance at the same time. These are the steps in order:

Step One
Stand with your feet slightly under shoulders' width apart.

Step Two
Elongate your spine and assume good posture.

Step Three
Stand with your weight slightly forward in your stance, concentrated on the balls of your feet.

Step Four
Let your arms rest naturally at your sides.

Bonus: S

Set the Stage for Speaking Success

THIS BONUS SECTION provides logistical reminders for getting your next business presentation off to a successful start.

Date of the presentation
- Has the date been published correctly in all of your promotional materials?
- Does the day of the week match the day of the month, and is the year correct?
- Does this group prefer *TWT meetings*? That's Tuesday, Wednesday, Thursday. Some organizations avoid scheduling events on Mondays and Fridays.
- Are you scheduling on the day before or after a holiday such as the Fourth of July?
- Have you considered vacation schedules when planning events?

Time considerations
- How long will your presentation run?
- Does the group prefer morning or afternoon meetings?
- Have you planned for "bio break" times throughout long meetings?

  Breaks are an important consideration. One technical client in Spartanburg, South Carolina, requires I slot a 10-minute break at the end of every professional development hour. It is their human resource policy as their employees are involved in high-stress jobs. So we work for 50 minutes and break for 10 minutes, work for 50 minutes and break for 10 minutes. It's a pattern I must build into my training agenda when I'm on their site.

- Have you allowed at least 10 minutes of margin to facilitate discussions and questions?
- Should you start a three-hour meeting at 10 a.m? (Not unless you're planning to provide lunch!)

Location

- Where will the session be held?
- Is there room availability?
- What size space will you need?
- Have you checked out the site ahead of time?

Hint: It's a great idea to keep a journal or notebook of your observations of the lighting, audio-visual equipment availability, quality of service, room size, noise level, etc., especially if you plan to return to that location for your next presentation.

Room setup

- Conference room table?
- Round tables?
- U-shaped seating?
- Auditorium style?
- Classroom style?
- Chevron style?
- Lighting?
- Room set up with posters, colorful charts, flip chart sheets, etc., to create an energy-generating atmosphere?
- Can everyone see you and the screen?

Make sure you speak the same language as the audio-visual professionals working with you. This quick vocabulary tip could save some confusion. Don't erroneously call the lectern a podium. The *lectern* is the speaker stand, the piece of furniture some speakers stand behind and place their notes. The *podium* is the platform on which you stand.

Possible presentation materials

- Microphone: wireless lavaliere or attached to lectern?

- Lectern?
- Flip chart paper and stand?
- Colored scented markers?
- Writing utensils?
- Handouts for participants?
- LCD projector?
- TV/DVD player setup?
- Dry-Erase® boards?
- Display tables?
- Tape?
- Master copies of presentation materials?
- Extra copies of all materials?
- Name tents/nametags?
- Music?
- Remote control?
- Laser pointer?
- Laptop computer and presentation software?
- Props and other visual aids?
- Door prizes and candy?
- Extension cords/extra three-pronged adapter?
- Back-up batteries?
- Emergency clothing?

Meeting snacks and meals

- Will you provide the refreshments, or will someone else be responsible for that detail?
- When will you serve snacks: during the presentation or at breaks?
- Have you considered appropriate foods and drinks for maintaining a high-energy level?

Paying attention to these details sets the stage for a successful presentation. *Chapter O: Own the Room* and *Chapter P: Pack Your Bags* delve more deeply into meeting preparation and execution.

"Tell them what you're going to tell them.
Tell them.
Tell them what you told them."

Madison Avenue approach

T

Tell Them What You're Going to Tell Them

THE MADISON AVENUE approach is especially effective for last-minute presentations when you have to organize your thoughts quickly. You really can't go wrong with it in a pinch. The "Tell Them What You're Going to Tell Them" aspect prompts speakers to pay special attention to how they plan to hook their audience at the beginning and open with oomph.

Good openings are sure-fire crowd pleasers. **Chapter M** touched on the three elements of good opening comments. Now it's time to delve deeper with these "must-do's" for any presentation opening in order:

1. Hook them with a relevant attention-grabbing device
2. Preview the purpose of your presentation
3. Give them a reason to listen, the benefits to them

Hook them with a relevant attention-grabbing device

Open strong by incorporating one of these attention-grabbing devices:

Tell a story with which the audience can relate

Most everyone enjoys a good story. I begin my grammar program with the story of the "Missing Comma on the Birthday Cake." People remember this funny comma trauma years later and even call me the "Comma Lady."

Share some startling statistics—no boring ones allowed

"More than 35 percent of business professionals have admitted to checking their e-mail in the bathroom." That's how I start my **Getting a Grip on E-mail @ Work** class.

Read the newspaper

Scour the local paper that morning for a relevant news story that interestingly may tie into your presentation, even loosely. It demonstrates you're aware of their corporate culture and local community. And it's fresh; it shows you don't go around giving the same canned speech at every location.

Ask an open-ended question

Expect answers. Get them talking to you. Remember, in many cases people would rather hear themselves talk than you, so by starting with more of them and less of you, you show a true desire to make your presentation relevant to their unique needs.

BLUF it

That is: <u>B</u>ottom <u>L</u>ine <u>U</u>p <u>F</u>ront. "As a result of our 30-minute presentation, you will walk away with a script for securing more direct sales, so let's dive straight into our content."

Ask a rhetorical question to get them thinking

"What makes a great presenter—you know, the ones who really stand out in your mind?" "What would it take to reach out to the 63 percent of families in our county who don't have a church home, and is this a realistic endeavor?"

Open with a meaningful visual aid

I begin my proofreading seminar with a slide of highway workers painting SOTP on the road at a school's crosswalk. It's a true example of lack of focus and ties directly to discussing the perils of multitasking while proofreading.

Involve someone in a demonstration

Quote someone in authority

Start with a show-of-hands opportunity

Use humor, though not necessarily a joke

Preview the purpose of the presentation

As a reminder, there are two categories of business presentations: action presentations and information presentations. Action presentations are developed around the questions: "What do I want my audience to do?" "How do I want my audience to feel?" Action presentations are written and presented because you want your recipients to do something as a result of hearing it or to act in some way differently as a result of being there. Be sure to articulate your call to action or the challenge you'll invoke in your opening. People like to hear language such as, "There are two requests I'll make of you tonight." Sales presentations are definitely action-oriented presentations, so don't be afraid to ask for the sale. Ask early; ask often. That's the defining purpose of your presentation to that group on that day; of course, you are going to follow with the many benefits to them for saying "yes."

Information presentations answer the question: "What do I want my audience to know?" Presenters don't necessarily want their audience members to *do* something as a result of hearing what they have to say. They simply want their target audience to *know* something they

183

perhaps didn't know about before, or they want them to *understand* a subject better. True informational presentations center on the classic lead sentence. The lead sentence answers the six journalist's questions, the five W's and the one H: the *who, what, when, where, why,* and *how*. Purposeful language in your opening explains: "There are two exciting time-saving advantages with our new accounting software system."

Give them reasons to listen, benefits to them

Spell these out clearly. Many times we assume the benefits are common sense, that they should be crystal clear to those listening. They may be clear to us but may not be as evident to our audience.

Our audience tunes into radio station WII-FM: <u>W</u>hat's <u>I</u>n <u>I</u>t <u>F</u>or <u>M</u>e. It is the station in life through which we filter everything. Our meeting participants are definitely tuned in to that channel at the beginning of the presentation, and it's our job through sharing benefits to keep them tuned in. We don't want to give them a good reason to change the channel.

Uncover the audience's benefit by asking "so what" about your topic twice. I have to assess this honestly for my topics. Why would anyone really be interested in attending a business writing seminar? It's not simply to be a better writer. The real benefits are deeper. It may look like this:

Why would you want to register for this business writing class?

To be a better writer at work.

So what?
It takes me way too long to write a letter, so I want to save time and write faster.

So what?
That way I have time to do what I'm really hired to do. I can invest in more high-value activities.

What might cause listeners to tune us out? Here are a few opening killers. Use them and you'll lose them.

- Apologizing
    - For being late
    - For not being as prepared as you should be
    - For being boring
    - For being underdressed
    - For microphone failure
    - For audio-visual equipment failure
- Simply repeating the presentation's title: BOR-ING
- The standard "Good morning, ladies and gentlemen and distinguished guests"
    - Every other speaker at the conference will do this, so stand out by opening with oomph and immediately hooking their interest.
- An unrelated and poorly delivered joke
- "It's so good to be here" fluff
    - Once I was attending a conference where the keynote speaker spent more than 20 minutes talking about how great it was to be in that city, how wonderful the restaurants were, and how he wasn't expecting it to be as cool there at night as it was. The woman seated next to me turned and said, "I live here; I didn't pay money to hear him talk about how good the food is and give me a weather report." Our audiences are time savvy and not very patient with fluff and filler. They want to know what we know; they want us to get to the point. They have people to see, places to go, things to do.
- Slow opening that drags on and on and doesn't get to the point quickly
- Complaining about the room setup, poorly working microphone, the cold temperature in the room, or any other meeting detail
- Something totally off the cuff
    - As Zig Ziglar advises: "If it ain't on the page, then it ain't on the stage." The beginning of your speech is no time for weak small talk. Nor is it the time to tell people the great joke you just heard out in the hallway two minutes earlier. If you haven't prepared to say it, resist the temptation to do so.

Instead, when you have a strong opening that you've practiced and can speak with confidence no matter what your circumstances, you'll immediately win your audience's attention. Start strong and end even stronger.

Now what?

Write out your opening statement word for word. Script it and work on it so you can open with great eye contact and without looking at your notes. Check it for the three must-have opening components: the attention-grabbing hook, the purpose, and the benefits to the audience to give them a good reason to listen. Tell them what you're going to tell them.

The NO-PANIC PLAN *for Presenters*

 ## Opening with Oomph Checklist
Must Do's in the Opening

1. The attention-grabbing hook

Script out your hook here. Perhaps choose from this list:

- ❏ Tell a story with which the audience can relate
- ❏ Share some startling statistics
- ❏ Tie in a current newsworthy event
- ❏ Ask an open-ended question and expect answers
- ❏ BLUF it
- ❏ Ask a rhetorical question to get them thinking
- ❏ Use a meaningful visual aid
- ❏ Involve someone in a demonstration
- ❏ Quote someone in authority
- ❏ Start with a show-of-hands opportunity
- ❏ Use humor, though not necessarily a joke
- ❏ _____

2. The preview of the presentation's purpose

_____

_____

3. The benefits and reasons for listening

_____

_____

Steer clear of these opening killers:

- ▪ Apologizing for anything up front
- ▪ Simply repeating the presentation's title
- ▪ Using the standard "Good morning, ladies and gentlemen and distinguished guests"
- ▪ Telling an unrelated and poorly delivered joke
- ▪ Starting with the "It's so good to be here" fluff
- ▪ Delaying getting to the point soon enough
- ▪ Complaining about anything
- ▪ Saying something totally off the cuff

Consider these design guidelines for preparing
crisp, clean, and consistent visual aids.

CHAPTER

Unclutter Your Slides

WE'VE ALL HEARD the running jokes about PowerPoint®. Business-people lament excruciatingly slow and painful "death by PowerPoint®." Organizations threaten to become PowerPoint-less. As soon as the lights go out for the slideshow, the eyes go closed for a nap!

Been there; done that. However, I feel compelled to rush to PowerPoint®'s defense. I'm a proud user of the slide presentation software and others like it. While most in this reading audience will be familiar with PowerPoint® and Keynote®, there are numerous other slideshow presentation programs for which these pointers will apply. For the sake of reader-friendliness of the following bullet points, I will refer to these with the generic word "slides."

Let's start with this list of slideshow pet peeves sales executives and other professional presenters complain about in the ***No-Panic Presentation Skills*** seminars.

- Boring
- Too much information on one slide
- Too hard to read
- Font too small
- Boring
- Unprofessional "cheesy" clip art
- Entire presentation scripted on the slides
- Speaker just read off the slides
- Boring
- Weak choice of background and font colors
- Spinning slides and moving text
- Transitions that are too elaborate
- Boring

Once these weak elements have been exposed, we all can improve our approach to designing these slides. ***Chapter R: Rehearse. Rehearse. Rehearse.*** revealed practical pointers for delivery of the slide presentation; this section sticks to slide design.

Slide design

Slides are designed to be visual aids, with emphasis on the word *aid*. They should complement what you're saying, not *be* what you're saying. In other words, you should make your point verbally and reinforce it with the slide, not the opposite approach. Yet, that's how so many presenters start: they see the slides as being the primary part of the presentation. Their message is the primary presentation; the slides are there to support and illustrate their words.

Once you've prepared your verbal presentation, crank up the computer and start designing your slides. Slides are ideal for highlighting:
- Line graphs to visually support your explanations
- Bar charts to show comparisons
- Pie charts to make statistics and percentages come to life
- Flow charts for explaining processes

- Photos that reflect the story you are telling
- Various cartoons and funny, unusual photographs used with permission to wake up your audience from time to time
- Any other illustrations to support your main point
- And of course, bulleted lists

Bulleted lists. I'm a big fan—when they're formatted correctly. In fact, I hope people will join me in the campaign to rid the world of bad bullets. No more 19 bullets crammed onto one slide. No more bulleted lists written in 10-point font size for a slide. No more inconsistently worded bullets. Instead, follow the **6 x 6 rule** for bulleted lists. Strive for no more than six bullets per slide with no more than six words per line.

Here are five great guidelines for wording bulleted lists. Check out this poorly written and punctuated example first.

Follow these instructions to select a background design:
- *select the Template option;*
- *double click the OK button;*
- *highlight the name of your choice; and*
- *the Apply button should be clicked.*

This example violates all five bulleted list guidelines. The first writing rule for bulleted lists is parallelism. Each item in a bulleted list must be parallel with the others, be there two bullets or 12 bullets in the list. To be parallel means the bulleted items have the same grammatical structure. They either all need to be phrases, or they all need to be complete sentences. You should not mix and match and be inconsistent in the same list. In the example above, three of the bullets begin with action verbs, and the last one is a passive voice sentence. To correct the faulty parallelism, just change the wording of the last one so that it now reads:

Follow these instructions to select a background design:
- *select the Template option;*
- *double click the OK button;*
- *highlight the name of your choice; and*
- *click the Apply button.*

Another question I'm asked in classes is, "Mandi, how do you punctuate bulleted lists?" Many of us have seen the above approach with either semicolons or commas used after each bullet. Current trends reflect open punctuation for bulleted lists. This means you don't need to include semicolons after each point; you don't need to use commas. You don't even need to place a period at the end of the last bullet. The mindset now is that bullets take the place of the ending punctuation. Indeed, the only punctuation mark you need is the colon after the introductory sentence to set up the list. Colons tell readers to keep reading; there's more to come. If a colon could walk up to you on the street and start talking to you, it would say, "Look out, something's following me." So, our newly punctuated example reflects open punctuation like this:

Follow these instructions to select a background design:
- *select the Template option*
- *double click the OK button*
- *highlight the name of your choice*
- *click the Apply button*

There is one exception to this rule. Sometimes your bulleted lists contain complex information that must be explained by multiple-sentence bullets. When you have more than one sentence per bullet, you use periods at the end of each one. You still use the colon to introduce it. Here's an example:

Quarterly update for company reveals:
- *While revenues grow, costs (due to fuel) rise exponentially, decreasing the profit seen by the company. EPS was $.05.*
- *Weather has also severely impacted revenues throughout the quarter.*
- *The company focused on additional capacity compared with last year's loads.*
- *A decreasing import market has begun to impact revenues and barge movements. Expectations for an aging equipment supply have lowered the stock price.*

Two bulleted points were addressed with multiple sentences, thereby requiring periods after all of them. To maintain parallel punctuation, all were worded as complete sentences with the period at the end. It is easy to see how on this slide each bulleted point lends itself to more detailed verbal explanations from the presenter; the bullet simply serves as a springboard to dive into more detail and perhaps supporting graphs and charts.

A discussion of punctuation naturally leads to the question of capitalization. Do you or don't you capitalize the first letter of the first word of each bulleted point in the list? The answer is *yes*. Regardless of the bullet structure, you do capitalize the first letter of the first word of each bullet, even if it's just a phrase or even a laundry list of ideas.

I even follow these bulleted list guidelines for my grocery lists.

If I might fly my geek flag up the pole for just a minute, I even follow these bulleted list guidelines for my grocery lists. After all, I would hate for my shopping list to fall into the hands of someone who would think I don't know appropriate punctuation and capitalization, so I even capitalize the items when compiling my list.

Shopping List for June 12
- *Apples*
- *Green onions*
- *Whole-wheat bread*
- *Granola bars*
- *Sour cream*
- *Chocolate chips*
- *Pickle relish*
- *Pretzels*

Yes, that is the correct bulleted formatting for a grocery shopping list! For larger lists, I might use headings such as "Produce" and "Dairy Products" to categorize my bullets in aisle-by-aisle order.

From our original example, here's how it looks now:

> *Follow these instructions to select a background design:*
> - *Select the Template option*
> - *Double click the OK button*
> - *Highlight the name of your choice*
> - *Click the Apply button*

Another question that arises in my seminars concerns the difference between numbering lists and using the bullet icons. There is a rule that governs this decision as well. Only use numbers when the items must be performed in order. Numbers indicate sequence and order of importance. We shouldn't just arbitrarily number lists, as in:

> *You need five ingredients for this recipe:*
> 1. *One box of butter-flavored cake mix*
> 2. *One cup water*
> 3. *¾ cup oil*
> 4. *Three eggs*
> 5. *One can of coconut pecan frosting*

No, if the items are of equal importance, use bullets. Numbers in this case would be used to indicate the order of preparation.

> *You need five ingredients for this recipe:*
> - *One box of butter-flavored cake mix*
> - *One cup water*
> - *¾ cup oil*
> - *Three eggs*
> - *One can of coconut pecan frosting*
>
> 1. *Mix all ingredients well*
> 2. *Pour into a greased Bundt pan*
> 3. *Bake at 300 degrees for one hour*

Our original example should be numbered because those steps must be performed in order like so:

Follow these instructions to select a background design:
1. *Select the Template option*
2. *Double click the OK button*
3. *Highlight the name of your choice*
4. *Click the Apply button*

At last, how many bullets must you have? At least two. Make sure you don't have any slides with just one bullet. In my line of work, we call those "stray bullets." You want to edit your slides for any stray bullets such as this one:

Training Effectiveness

- *Reviewed effectiveness reports for last quarter's training and indicated areas for improvement*

Remove the bullet and tweak the information into a sentence format. The rules for bullets reflect the rules we **In my line of work, we call those "stray bullets."** learned in the fourth grade for Roman numeral outlines: You can't have an A. without a B. You can't have a 1. without a 2. You should not have one bullet on the screen unless there is another.

As a bonus guideline for formatting bulleted lists, especially for procedures and action-oriented bulleted information, follow the **1=1 Rule**: One bullet = One physical movement. This helps you determine how many bullets you really need, and it stifles the tendency to cram too much information into one bulleted sentence. Remember the **1=1 Rule** when crafting bulleted lists for your slides.

Font selection is another decision to make when designing slides. There are two font families: serif and sans serif. Serif fonts include Times New Roman, Garamond, and Bookman Old Style. They have the hooks and feet on the letters. Sans serif fonts are sleek without the hooks and feet: Arial, Verdana, Tahoma, and Trebuchet are common examples of sans serif fonts. Sans serif fonts are preferred for slides. They stand out on the slides and are easier to read from a distance in various color combinations. You especially want to use a sans serif font for the bold heading on each slide.

Sizes should be customized for your audience. Most slide presentation programs default to 44-point for the headings and 32-point for the body copy and bullets. In essence, there's never a reason these days to say, "Now this slide may be a little hard to read."

In essence, there's never a reason these days to say, "Now this slide may be a little hard to read."

For slideshow presentations, stay away from the amateurish white slides with black text. Graphic designers recommend these combinations for maximum readability and depth of color:

- Green background with white writing

    That's the color pairing for our U.S. highway road signs: it's readable from long distances at fast speeds.

- Blue background with white writing
- Black background with yellow writing

Simply switching to one of these color choices will professionalize your slideshow more so than black on white.

Final slide production pointers include:

- Don't get fancy with bouncing bullet point entrances and spinning slide transitions. Just because you *can* do it doesn't mean you *should*.
- Remember to include your contact information and/or logo on each slide. Emulate how television stations include their small emblem in the bottom right-hand portion of the screen throughout the show you're watching.
- Have a montage of slides projecting on the screen as people enter the meeting.
- Put a lot of thought into the last slide. If it is an action-oriented presentation, does the slide show people exactly what to do next? If it is a sales presentation, do you use your final slide to ask for the sale? Does it wrap the total presentation up in a neat package with a

bow on top? Have you included the essential information you want your audience to walk away with after the meeting adjourns? Is your name and contact information on the final slide as well?

- Take advantage of technology and use short meaningful video clips throughout your slideshow to reinforce the point you are making.

Now what?

Review your current slide presentation and implement a few of the pointers in this chapter. You don't have to make a lot of changes at first, but even doing something as simple as changing your font style or reversing the colors of your slides or even rethinking the approach you take with your closing slide can update and freshen the visual representation of your presentation.

Can you identify your favorite vocal fillers?
Better yet, can someone else tell you?

CHAPTER

Voice Your Vocal Concerns

OUCH! Lesson Learned the Hard Way

A participant in one of my seminars in Portland, Maine, approached me at the morning break to ask me, "Did you know you said the word 'particular' six times during your presentation? The word 'particular' adds absolutely no value to your sentence. It's a wasted word." Ouch. Yet, I've always remembered that—and I haven't uttered the word "particular" since!

OUCH! Lesson Learned the Hard Way

Years ago, a college professor embarrassed me in front of the entire communication class. The more I sit here and think about it, it still stings a little today. We were talking about wording issues and improvements in a mock presentation for a business proposal. The script in question began: "Pursuant to our previous discussion...." I spoke up and recommended rewording it, "Per our discussion." Without missing a beat, my professor responded, "Mandi, only cats 'per.'" Students snickered. The teacher just laughed. Perhaps that's why I haven't used the word "per" in 20 years.

Perhaps it's also why I don't own a cat.

One of my speech teachers called these issues vocal garbage or vocal trash. They include:
- Vocal fillers
- "Favorite" words
- Poor pitch
- Rapid rate
- Monotone delivery

How do you discover these vocal crutches in your presentation? There's only one way I know for sure: tape yourself. You're not aware of how you sound to others until you hear it for yourself. It's about as enjoyable of hearing your own voice message on your phone's answering machine, but it works. I coached one candidate running for state senate who followed this advice. We taped his presentation; he waited 48 hours and then listened to it. When we had our next coaching session two days later, he presented his entire stump speech without a single "um" or "uh." Marveled by such a drastic turnaround with his delivery, I asked how he had cleaned out all of his pesky vocal fillers so quickly. He said, "I counted the number of 'ums' and 'uhs' as you recommended, and it made me sick. I had no idea I used so many fillers, so I decided to clean them out cold turkey and not be afraid to have pauses in the places where I was substituting sounds. It just sounded so unprofessional, and I think it diminished the power behind the ideas I'm espousing." He was elected.

It's about as enjoyable of hearing your own voice message on your phone's answering machine, but it works.

Vocal fillers

Vocal fillers include "um," "uh," "ah," continual throat clearing, gulping or constant swallowing, and lip smacking. One professional speaking organization rings a bell every time a speaker utters a vocal filler; another group drops a nail in a bucket with a loud clang whenever someone carelessly inserts a filler sound.

"Favorite" words

I had no clue I used the word "particular" so much until that participant pointed it out to me. Then I realized I made comments such as "on this particular page of your workbook" or "in this particular example" or "on this particular slide." Other favorite filler phrases can be:

- "You know"
- "Like"
- "Like, you know"
- "And"
- "The point is"
- "Well"
- "Basically"
- "Okay"
- "At the end of the day"

When my first son was no older than three, he prefaced almost every other sentence with the word "actually." He distinctly pronounced each syllable, and it sounded so funny coming out of a three-year-old's mouth: "Actually, I want to read this book." "Actually, spaghetti would be good for supper." Another fabulous speaker I enjoy hearing has two favorite phrases: "oftentimes" and "quite frankly." He has no idea he uses them so much. Sometimes a friend or coworker can point out your favorite words.

Poor pitch

When listening to your tape, pay attention to your pitch. Anxiety and even the adrenaline pumping through your body prior to standing up to speak result in a higher-than-normal pitch. This can lessen your credibility and authority with a group, especially if you are a woman.

Rapid rate

That same adrenaline can result in a much more-rapid-than-usual rate of speech. I once had someone in New York comment on an evaluation: "She's the fastest talking Southerner I've ever heard." I don't think it was a compliment.

Monotone delivery

If you have a tendency to go monotone when presenting information, practice more inflection and even changing your facial expression to incorporate more energy and feeling.

If you don't sound interested in what you're saying, your audience certainly won't be.

If you don't sound interested in what you're saying, your audience certainly won't be. Monotone equals boring. Having a monotone delivery is one of the biggest speaker turnoffs among conference goers, who certainly don't like to sit in a dark room and feel as if the presenter is just phoning it in.

Now what?

Tape your presentation and listen to yourself without the video component. Pay "particular" attention to any vocal fillers, favorite words and phrases, poor pitch, rapid rate, and monotone delivery.

Take care of your voice:

- Avoid consuming dairy foods prior to speaking as they produce throat congestion.
- Stay away from caffeine and alcohol as well; they rob the body of moisture.
- Drink plenty of room-temperature water. Nix the ice as it restricts the vocal cords.
- Warm up your voice while out of sight of audience members. Begin by stretching your mouth muscles with a deep yawn. As unattractive as this may sound, produce some saliva and swallow it. Repeat that two or three times. Clear your throat once or twice, and choose a vocal repetition workout such as articulating "me, they, me, they, me, they" or the tongue-twister of your choice such as "rubber baby buggy bumpers."

"I believe more in scissors than I do the pencil."
Truman Capote

■ ■ ■

"Never use a big word when a diminutive alternative can be utilized."
Unknown

■ ■ ■

"The most valuable of all talents is that of never
using two words when one will do."
Thomas Jefferson

■ ■ ■

"A person who is to make a speech at any time anywhere or upon
any topic owes it to himself and to his audience to write it out."
Mark Twain

■ ■ ■

"To communicate, put your thoughts in order; give them a purpose;
use them to persuade, to instruct, to discover, to seduce."
William Safire

Wow Them with Your Wording

GONE ARE THE DAYS of the old three-points-and-a-poem speech-writing formula. Instead, consider this tried-and-true organizational template for any presentation, be it a technical presentation, a sales call, a budget report, or even a pep talk:

1. Opening
2. Body
3. Closing

In **Chapter M: Memorize Your First and Last Sentences**, we delved into how to write powerful openings with these three key ingredients: an attention-grabbing device, the purpose of the presentation, and the benefit to the audience to give them a reason for listening. We listed several attention-grabbing devices designed to open with oomph:

- Tell a great opening story to which the audience can relate
- Ask a provocative rhetorical question
- Ask an open-ended question—and expect answers

- Share some startling statistics—no boring ones allowed
- Use humor, though not necessarily a joke
- Quote someone interesting
- Read the newspaper and tie in a newsworthy current event
- Involve them in a pair-and-share exercise or other immediate relevant activity off of which you can build your message
- BLUF your audience; give them the <u>B</u>ottom <u>L</u>ine <u>U</u>p <u>F</u>ront
- Begin with a series of "How many of you have ever...?" questions where they can respond by raising their hands
- Involve someone in a demonstration
- Simply do something to get them to nod in agreement or shake their heads in disbelief
- Open with a meaningful visual aid

In **Chapter C** we learned to dissect closing statements for these three elements: the closing signal, the summary statement, and the big bang. That chapter listed proven methods for closing with conviction:

- Ending with questions that challenge your participants
- Using a final personal anecdote or good story you have saved for the end
- Finishing with a short yet meaningful quotation
- Using one last bold fact or startling statistic
- Repeating the one big idea
- Relating your main point to a current newsworthy event
- Invoking your call to action
- Creatively circling back to your opening statements
- Tying everything together with a fitting and well-planned analogy

The opening of your speech and the closing are covered. What about the body? There are countless ways to format the body of your presentation. I will list a few easy-to-organize methods for you and reveal my favorite approach at the end. Use any one of them to wow the people in your next meeting.

Numeric approach

This one is easy, especially if asked to give an impromptu presentation with only a few minutes to collect your thoughts. This approach makes titling your presentation a no-brainer as well: "Seven Steps to Speaking Success," "Three Tips and Techniques for Technical Writing," "Five Goals for our Organization in the New Year." Odd numbers seem to resonate with listeners, yet I would strive to keep the number seven and below. Very few people want to sit down and suddenly hear they're going learn about "19 Methods for Developing Leaders."

Story-point-story

Sandwich your main point between two memorable stories, and people will walk out of your meeting much more likely to remember what you said. People may not remember your main point, but if they can remember the story, that will trigger memory of the point supported by the story.

Acrostic method

This one is as easy as ABC. Here's an example: In my proofreading seminar, I teach the primary approach to proofreading, which is called the newspaper proof. After the class practices the newspaper proof, we turn the page to some complementary proofreading suggestions. I categorize them as the START strategy:

S   Spell check the document
T   Tag team
A   Approach line by line
R   Read out loud
T   Take a break

Goals and actions

This definitely is designed for action presentations and is a good formula for speaking up at team meetings, strategic planning sessions, and even when you are charged with presenting your idea to a group of key decision makers. You simply explain your goal and step by step walk through the action plan to achieve it.

Chronological order

With this approach you use a timeline to anchor your main points. It's up to you if you want to start at the beginning and work toward the present and future or start with the present and work backward.

My favorite: One point only

If your audience can walk away with just one key message, what would that be in one sentence? Realistically speaking, your audience won't remember all five points of your speech—or even three points for that matter. But if you can drill down your message to one key take-away and reinforce that main idea with stories, statistics, testimonials, and visual aids, then if someone is asked the next day what your meeting was about, they are more likely to rattle off the main point exactly as you presented it. I strive to chisel out the one main point and then support it at least two or three ways.

Now what?

Record your speaking successes. As soon as possible after a presentation, write down which organizational approach you used, the interactives you used to support your main purpose, what went well, and what changes you would make the next time, if any.

The NO-PANIC PLAN *for Presenters*

 ## My Speaking Success Recorder

Record your presentation success stories here.

When a joke gets a lot of laughs, or a demonstration works extremely well, or you word a main point in a way you wish to remember, or your ending story is a big hit with your audience, capture the details here so you can repeat them in later presentations.

❏ Date of presentation _____

❏ Location_____

❏ Company or audience_____

❏ Title of presentation_____

_____

❏ Which technique worked well? _____

_____

_____

❏ Which main point did it support? _____

_____

_____

❏ How did you word it? _____

_____

_____

❏ What changes, if any, will you make for your next presentation? _____

_____

_____

_____

_____

_____

"Truth is stranger than fiction."
Mark Twain

Xpect the Unexpected

NOT TOO LONG AGO, I sent the following letter to a hand-selected group of some of the best professional speakers I know:

> *Dear Speaker,*
>
> *In Chapter X of my upcoming book, I'm highlighting personal examples from well-known professional speakers of how ANYTHING CAN HAPPEN in an executive presentation setting and how the show must go on.*
>
> *Would you be willing to share a fitting example from your career exemplifying how important it is to "Xpect the Unexpected" and how you learned from it? It can be either a success story of how you overcame the unexpected situation, or it can be a big flop, a lesson learned the hard way.*
>
> *Sincerely,*
>
> *Mandi*

What I received in response absolutely blew me away! I genuinely was overwhelmed by the generosity of the following folks who shared their speaking nightmares and funny stories.

May you enjoy and learn from the following personal accounts as much as I did.

Mark Sanborn's story

Think of a time you were about to make a very important presentation. Once you do, you'll understand how I felt when I was about to address the leaders of a global consulting practice.

The audience was populated with high-level executives, and if I nailed the presentation the potential for more speaking business was great. Every speech gets my best effort, but this was a time to do an extraordinary job.

The morning of the presentation I cut myself shaving.

I don't mean I nicked myself or that I bled a little. It was more like I opened an artery. I started bleeding quite profusely and couldn't stop. A septic pencil didn't work, nor did the little pieces of tissue paper. Frankly, I don't think an entire roll of toilet paper would have helped much. Even prayer seemed ineffective at that point. I simply had to apply pressure and wait for the bleeding to cease.

Thankfully, it did stop about an hour before I took the stage. I was grateful.

I was introduced, took the stage, and started having fun. The speech was going very well.

That was until I felt a trickle on the side of my face. I wasn't sweating that much, so I was fearful. My suspicion was confirmed by a woman in the front row whose eyes were rolling up into her head as if she were about to pass out. Evidently, she was squeamish about blood.

Every speaker has bled on stage at some point in his or her career, but it was only figuratively. This was literal. Not only had I never experienced this before, I hadn't even anticipated it.

What to do? I had limited options. I simply removed my handkerchief from my pocket and applied pressure. At the same time I acknowledged and apologized for the situation. I continued speaking, and before I finished my speech, I was able to joke about the unusual circumstance.

I know this sounds odd, and I can't prove it, but I think it is possible the audience liked me better because of my on-stage bleeding.

Why? Because we're all human, and that means we're imperfect. Stuff happens, and we empathize when we see someone dealing with a challenging situation because we all deal with things like that all the time. Author Anne Lamott says, 'There's nothing funnier on earth than our humanness and our monkeyness. There's nothing more touching.'

But, we also like to see someone handle a difficult situation well (or at least as well as it can be handled). I made the most of the cards I had been dealt by acknowledging and apologizing. I didn't try to cover it up, and in this case, I couldn't have even if I had tried. With a little time and understanding, we eventually can laugh at things that aren't initially funny, sometimes sooner than later.

I bled on stage. I couldn't anticipate nor could I avoid what happened— although I do shave a little more carefully these days. My humbling situation only proved my humanity, and that's not a bad thing at all.

Mark Sanborn, CSP, CPAE Speaker Hall of Fame
President
Sanborn & Associates, Inc., an idea studio for leadership development
Past president of the National Speakers Association
www.MarkSanborn.com

Naomi Rhode's story

As a platform professional, it is important to remember that the person with the microphone has the power, leadership, and responsibility for what happens during their platform presence.

Another tenant is certainly true as well: "If it can happen, it may happen."

Speaking on leadership before a group of several hundred business-people, I had the responsibility of modeling leadership skills in a time of crisis. Midpoint through my keynote address, a woman in the front row had an epileptic seizure.

I was able to say calmly, "Is there a medical professional in the room? We have an emergency in the front row."

Immediately, two people came forward: one a nurse and the other trained as a paramedic. I then suggested that everyone else in the room just quietly bow their heads and say a silent prayer for the woman in the front row. It was very quiet. The trained people helped the woman, determined we did not need to call paramedics, and escorted her out into the lobby.

I thanked the audience for caring about the situation and continued talking about leadership with a new and current example of the importance of knowing what to do, and then empowering your team to do it with you.

The rest of the story is that the audience had a very interesting bond for the remainder of the session. Everyone was attentive, involved, and "present"—more so than before because they had been part of a team to restore order and health midst an unexpected trauma.

Naomi Rhode, CSP, CPAE Speaker Hall of Fame
Cofounder, SmartHealth
Past president of the National Speakers Association

Past president of the Global Speakers Federation
1997 Cavett Award winner
2003 Legend of the Speaking Profession recipient
NaomiRhodeCPAE@gmail.com

Joe Turner's story

In addition to speaking, I am also a professional entertainer specializing in the mystery arts: magic, sleight of hand, mentalism, and illusions. I often integrate magic performances into my presentations to illustrate specific points.

For change management and leadership, one illustration I use is a famous card trick called "Any Card at Any Number." Many magicians consider this effect the "holy grail" of card magic. The effect is this: A spectator names a random card and a random number, and that card is then found at that position in the deck. I use it to illustrate a point about how leaders sometimes have to work behind the scenes to align different forces and circumstances in their organizations to achieve a goal. Without divulging any secrets, there are many methods to achieve this effect; the experienced performer often has to choose the method based on the environment, audience, and circumstances. That fact is also part of my message.

In one presentation I encountered a spectator who was somewhat more interactive than I had anticipated. In fact, he seemed more interested in proving he could prevent me from achieving the desired outcome than in grasping the point of the illustration. Whatever his motivation, he interrupted the presentation and insisted on inspecting the cards, shuffling them, and holding them so I couldn't do any sleight of hand with the deck.

I decided to let him do what he wanted. I have enough skill to accomplish what I need in a variety of ways, and I thought I could both defuse his mild belligerence and still make my point by letting him have a little rope.

He shuffled the cards, cut them, shuffled them again, and held them tight in his hands. He announced that he wanted the two of clubs to appear at position 26 and that he was going to deal the cards himself. I told him to deal 25 cards and set the 26th card aside without turning it over. He complied.

With all attention now on that card, I retook the rest of the deck and prepared for my alternate conclusion. As I spoke to the audience about the test conditions that had been imposed, I looked for the two of clubs. It wasn't there. I double checked. The two of clubs was not in the pack. As I slowly realized what had happened, I had a moment of glorious understanding, which I had to conceal from the audience. They were about to experience a piece of magic that I had not planned nor could I ever repeat for them. It was an unexpected bonus for them, but it was even more unexpected for me.

I recounted everything in order to help the audience cement their memories of what had happened, ensuring that they would be perfect witnesses to the strict conditions imposed. I snapped my fingers over the card and asked the man to show the audience the two of clubs.

There it was.

After a moment of stunned silence followed by a couple of shocked expletives, he said, "Okay, *that* was good. I have no idea." He then joined in the audience's applause.

For magicians, an "out" is an alternate conclusion—a back-pocket way to achieve a successful outcome even if it is different from what you intended when the trick began. Having outs is about having answers to all of the "what ifs" you can conceive. It's about going beyond your skill in your presentation and planning for numerous other skills that may never be seen by an audience except under unexpected conditions. It's about preparing a dozen or more ways to get from point A to point B, but any given audience will experience only one path. Neither they nor I can predict with perfect certainty which path it will be. I know that 99 percent of the time we'll be close to my expectations, but presentations are a form of live theater, and anything can happen.

By preparing outs, I was confident in my ability to walk down an alternate path to see where it would take both me and my audience. As a result of being prepared for an unexpected challenge, I was able to put myself in position to take advantage of an unexpected miracle—an "out" that I never could have executed with mere skill alone. It was a moment I'll never forget.

Joe M. Turner
Turner Magic Entertainment for corporate entertainment, keynotes, and seminars
www.TurnerMagic.com and www.TurnerTalks.com

Pamela Jett's story
Sometimes the sky really *is* falling.

As a professional speaker, I have experienced all sorts of challenges: falling off the platform—literally; microphones not working in front of huge crowds; rooms not being set adequately for the number of people, which results in crowded and cranky audience members; speaking in a barn—more than once; and having fire drills, power outages, and other unexpected events disrupt the flow of my presentations. Not one of these events, except falling off the stage, has been in my circle of influence or control. They were the responsibility of the meeting planner. Still, I've learned to handle most of these situations in what I believe to be a professional manner and give the audience a presentation that is valuable and worth their time and attention.

Of course, sometimes things happen that can tax even a professional's capacity to problem solve and exercise the "show-must-go-on" attitude meeting planners and clients expect.

It was in Anchorage, Alaska. The client opted to rent a hotel meeting room and had done a lovely job ensuring the room setup was great. Everything was going nicely for the first part of my presentation. Then, the unexpected occurred: a piece of ceiling fell on an audience member's head.

It had been snowing, and the roof had sprung a leak. This leak saturated the panels in the ceiling, and they came crumbling down in large chunks on a lovely woman's head in the back row. While shocked, she was not injured. However, this brought the meeting to a standstill. After I recovered from my momentary surprise, I realized the audience expected *me* to do something. Despite my not really being "in charge" and simply working for their boss as a hired speaker, the audience needed me to make a quick decision with respect to "what now?"

My decision was to ask her if she needed someone to call 911. Was she injured? Once learning she was not, I called a 15-minute break and immediately went to the hotel management and told them of the problem. Hotel management took over from there, moved us to another room, filed an incident report, etc.

What I learned from this situation is that even if you are not technically in charge of running the meeting, if you are speaking, the audience will expect you to take charge when the unexpected occurs. They will expect you to stay calm, cool, and collected. They will take their behavioral cues from you. If you become flustered or panic, they will become more nervous and upset. By staying calm and taking action, you maintain your credibility and professionalism in the eyes of your audience. This is true even if your version of taking charge is to calmly and confidently defer to the person running the meeting. In my case, I deferred to hotel management because the person who hired me was not in the room, and action had to be taken immediately.

Successful presenters take command at the front of the room. They are decisive and in charge from the platform. My advice to executive presenters is to be a calm and confident authority in the room, both in terms of your content and when the sky is falling!

Pamela Jett, CSP
Jett Communications
www.JettCT.com

Kimberly Medlock's story

I am a productivity expert. Among my accreditations is that I am certified as a professional organizer. It's not always easy being a certified professional organizer. I have to try harder than most to "keep my ducks in a row." As you might imagine, when you have this accreditation, you are much quicker to be scrutinized and judged by others on practically every aspect of orderliness and time management. I actually have had people come into my home and want to view my closets just to see if I really do what I say can be done.

However, as well as I do practice what I teach and walk the talk, nobody is perfect.

In March, I had a really important half-day presentation to a group at a Fortune 200 company about being productive. If you are a speaker, you know that no matter how good you are or how well you know your stuff, you still can get stressed about certain presentations. This was one of those instances. And if you are human, you also know that occasionally there are days when, as they say, you "get up on the wrong side of the bed" and anything that can go wrong will.

Now please understand I have been blissfully married to my husband Preston for 20 years, and we get along really well. However, this particular morning, I found myself giving him a lecture on "always waiting until the last minute" to get things done. I can't even remember now what the issue was at the time, but something had happened (or hadn't happened) that had caused me some kind of extra effort, and I wasn't happy about it. There were no blows, profanity, or anything like that.

It was more like one of those "why can't you just..." kind of talks. (Did I mention we have been blissfully married for 20 years?) Anyway, he respectfully took the lecture, and I left for my presentation.

I arrived on time, despite what seemed to be a ridiculous amount of traffic irritations. I took a deep breath, tried to center myself and shake off the frustrations of the morning. As I was setting up in the conference room, soon to be filled with 20 participants, I couldn't find my PowerPoint® CD. I typically create the outline and PowerPoint® on my desktop and then copy it to a CD to use in my laptop. This had worked well for me until now. "No! This can't be happening! It has to be here somewhere!" After I searched every nook and cranny of my bags, I had to face the fact that I forgot to pack the presentation CD. As I was fighting back a breakdown, I realized there was just one thing I could do. I had to call my husband and admit to him my mistake and ask for his help. Now that rush hour had passed, if he would just drop everything, grab the CD from my office, and rush like a crazy person, he could get here in time. He did—no questions asked.

I pulled myself together, the presentation went well, and the feedback was great. On the way back, despite feeling sheer exhaustion from the stress of the day, I remember specifically thinking about what I had learned from this day's events. One, *always* save a copy of the Power-Point® slides to my laptop. Two, eating crow stinks! But, I was blessed and grateful that at least this meal of crow would include a dessert hug and smile of forgiveness.

Kimberly Medlock, CPO
www.ProductiveMatters.com

Larry Mersereau's story

Last fall I was doing a breakout session for a large conference. About 15 minutes into the program, someone switched the sound system so the voice of a speaker in another room was coming through our room's speakers along with mine. My audience was not expecting a duet!

An alert participant went to find the meeting planner to get the situation corrected. In the meantime, for 20 minutes, I presented with the other speaker's voice echoing through the room with mine. For a while I even turned the sound system off altogether and talked at the top of my lungs. (Mom always said my voice carried.)

I worked very hard to use the visual part of my program, pointing to the screen and acting out parts whenever possible. I was trying everything.

There was a round of applause when the other speaker's voice finally went away, a standing ovation for me at the end of my program, and a wonderful letter of praise from the meeting planner a week later.

Ever since that program, I've looked at how I design my PowerPoint® slides completely differently. You never know when you might be presenting more visually than orally.

Larry Mersereau, CTC
www.PromoPower.com

Amanda Box's story

The Future Business Leaders of America was a popular club at Marshall County High School in Benton, Kentucky, so as a sophomore, I joined the group. Right away the sponsors recognized my talent for speaking and recruited me for the impromptu speaking competition at the FBLA convention. In preparation, I looked at some topics given to students in previous years, ran a few laps around the microphone, and pronounced myself ready. We loaded up on the jumbo yellow school bus, sans seat belts and security cameras, and headed to Murray State University for a day of FBLA adventure.

The time came for my session. I was handed my impromptu speech topic and given five minutes to prepare. Sweet! This was one I had already studied: *How do you make a good impression when starting a new job?* No problem. No only was I a prolific speaker, I actually HAD a job, bussing tables at Country Crossroads, a fish restaurant. I was doubly prepared after experiencing unprecedented bussing success and talking about how hard I worked all the time anyway.

I was anxious to get this gig wrapped up so I could get to the stage and pick up my big trophy. My turn came; I walked in.

There were three judges, but I really only remember one. He had wavy sandy brown hair parted on the side, was about 35, wore a corduroy jacket with a tie, and sat with his arms crossed over his chest. His face is what I really remember.

I began to talk on a significantly lower quality level than a normal speech. Then I digressed to stringing together some puny clichés. At this point, I concluded my five-minute planning period was flawed. From there, I began the humiliation of repetition, something about putting your best foot forward. I just silently begged God to let the time be up while I soaked in the judge's face. How could the first five minutes go so quickly and this five minutes go so slowly? Strangely, I still heard sounds of some sort coming out of my mouth, which was highly unlikely considering my stupidity-induced condition of dry mouth and low blood sugar coma.

Like I said, the judge's face is what I really remember. Nonverbal communication is normally 65-90 percent of all communication. This day it was 100 percent. His face said it all: "I am in severe pain, and you are causing it."

The trophy delusion was amply bludgeoned, and I scurried out of that room with a crucial lesson learned. Arrogance: It never fails to punish the transgressor. Yes, at 16 I was arrogant, but I haven't made that mistake since. Whether my presentation is five minutes or five hours, I am fully prepared. In my 20-year communication career, much of it has been spent with clients and students in public speaking training. I'm brilliant with shallow conversation after listening to thousands of three-to-five-minute speeches. The arrogance law still holds true. Nervousness doesn't ruin a speech, and blind confidence doesn't guarantee success.

Amanda Box
Owner of Amanda Box Communication
www.AmandaBox.net

Bobbe White's story

A hotel was having an employee rally as they were attempting to vie for a national award. They weren't able to pay my speaking fee in cash; however, they agreed to video tape my presentation and pay my travel expenses. It was a good tradeoff for me, or seemed to be, at the start. I touched base with the meeting planner in advance, and everything seemed to be in order. The employees would be treated to lunch before the program. Around 120 attendees were expected from managerial to custodial staff. I had visions of grandeur. If I could do a great job, this could be a snowball of success as I rolled into hundreds of other franchises in this hotel giant.

I entered the ballroom where the taco buffet and tables were set. The food smelled wonderful. The employees were in for a treat. I gave my handouts to the meeting planner and let her know I had translated about 20 of them into Spanish as we had discussed in my preprogram questionnaire. "Oh my goodness," she said, "That will NEVER be enough!" My blood ran cold. I wasn't sure how my program would work in a diverse group. The information quickly crystallized in my mind that the language barrier she spoke of was not just a casual comment but a major obstacle in their environment. Even though I am from a small midwestern community, I have traveled enough to know hotels in and around metropolitan areas employ diverse populations.

The theme of the rally was "Simply the Best!" A wonderful slide show capturing all employees, at their best, was set to music. It was a terrific ice breaker as many of the photos evoked laughter. The mayor said a few words of encouragement and congratulations, and all 12 owners of the franchise were present. The team was in place and ready to tape. Because I speak on incorporating humor in the workplace to manage stress—with some laughter therapy thrown in—I still felt hopeful it would be a hit. My stories fell flat. The room was completely quiet, except for the a/v guys who got my humor. I had crashed and burned fast. That was the bad news. Perhaps my video footage would still be visually usable. The good news, if any, was that when I segued into the laughter exercises, I realized that laughter is universal and needs no interpretation. While I ended on a better note, I still couldn't recover from the weak part of my program.

It was the longest program of my life. The video was horrible because I looked so frantic as I realized my ship was sinking. I was mad at myself for not having done my research on this group more deeply. The meeting planner gave me a clue, and I should have picked up on that information in advance. I simply didn't do my homework. While they were simply the best at what they did, I was simply the worst that day at what I did.

I called a speaker friend and mentor who listened to my saga. We began to laugh hysterically at my failure. What else could we do? She ended the call by saying, "Sometimes you're the star. Sometimes you're the taco meat!"

Bobbe White
Speaker, Author, Certified Laughter Leader (seriously!)
Try Laughter! Inc.
bobbe@trylaughter.com

Yet another story from Bobbe White
Punctuality is a perpetual challenge for some of us, especially when we try to run that one extra errand. Inevitably it is the errand that makes us late or run too close. I seem to do better with time when I am traveling to another time zone, which means I am flying to a speech. Airlines do not care if I am late, which means I play by their rules and not mine.

I was speaking for a hospital in my hometown for a community health program. It was a mere 20 blocks away. I also worked at a bank, so I would be speaking on my lunch hour for the most part. My mother, mother-in-law, and all their girlfriends would be in attendance to hear my speech for the first time, and I knew about 75 percent of the attendees as this was my hometown. I planned to take the back road for the 12:30 p.m. presentation in order to avoid the lunch-hour traffic. I left the bank at 11:45, and with a maximum of a 10-minute drive to the venue, I still had a cushion of 35 minutes. And, because I am a multi-tasker to the extreme, I also remembered that Crest White Strips® have about a 10-minute time span. So, at the first stoplight, I applied the upper strip and then the lower strip at the next stoplight. I was brilliant! My mothers would be so proud, and my smile would be dazzling.

When I pulled into the parking lot, it was already full, spilling over. Why were so many people here so early? It wasn't quite noon, and I was scheduled to speak at 12:30. I grabbed my bag, and the meeting planner met me outside. "We were so worried about you! Everyone's seated and ready to go at noon. Are you okay? Do you need anything? How much time do you need to set up?"

My mouth went to cotton as it normally does under stress. I still had my White Strips® on and lisped, "It tharth at noon? I thought it wath 12:30."

"Noon. Let's go. What do you need?"

"Thum water would be nithe."

Yep, there they all were: a couple hundred people from my own town, in place and waiting anxiously. My mother and mother-in-law were not sitting so tall all of a sudden, thinking, "Bobbe's late again. What will we do with that child?"

I did get started on time, with one minute to set up, remove the strips, and drink a cup of water. But, it wasn't the most impressive of starts to the meeting planner or audience. My program went well, but you never feel as if you recover when coming out of the starting blocks this abruptly.

As soon as we had a chance to compare notes, I admitted my time line was off about 30 minutes. Lisa, the planner, was just glad nothing had happened on the way. The only thing that happened is I learned yet another valuable lesson. I explained to Lisa why I needed the water so desperately. We had a good laugh over the fact that she would now call me Bobbe White Strips.

Bobbe White
Speaker, Author, Certified Laughter Leader (seriously!)
Try Laughter! Inc.
bobbe@trylaughter.com

✓ NO-PANIC Notes

"Research on the effectiveness of spoken communication and how a message is perceived by the audience reveals **55 percent** of the message is perceived from body language and facial expression, **38 percent** is perceived from voice tone and paralinguistics, and only **7 percent** is perceived from the words spoken."

Paraphrased communication study conducted by
Dr. Albert Mehrabian, Professor Emeritus of Psychology, UCLA

Remember: You and Your Audience are the Presentation

Dr. Mehrabian reminds us:

55 percent of our message is communicated through our body language and other cues

38 percent is communicated through our tone of voice

7 percent is communicated through our words

Now what?

Use this ***No-Panic Plan for Presenters*** every time to make sure your voice, posture, gestures, visuals, and even your dress are sending the message to your audience you desire.

"Everyone has butterflies in their stomach.
The only difference between a pro and an amateur
is the pro has them flying in formation."

Zig Ziglar

Heed <u>Z</u>ig <u>Z</u>iglar's Advice

OKAY, I'LL ADMIT: Z was a tough one. But I had the pleasure of sharing the stage with best-selling author and motivational speaker Zig Ziglar back in 1997 in Overland Park, Kansas. I'll never forget his positive energy and words of advice to other presenters: "Everyone has butterflies in their stomach. The only difference between a pro and an amateur is the pro has them flying in formation."

Now what?

Use this book to overcome the sweaty palms, shaky hands, quivering voice, and excessive nervous energy you may encounter before an important presentation—and they're *all* important. Take control of these A-to-Z elements, focus on the gift you're giving your audience rather than on yourself, and you'll get your "butterflies flying in formation."

After all, as Mr. Ziglar reminds us:

"Your attitude, not your aptitude, will determine your altitude."

Recommended Resources

Booher, Dianna. *Speak with Confidence: Powerful Presentations that Inform, Inspire, and Persuade.* New York, NY: McGraw-Hill, 2003.

Paulson, Terry, Ph.D. *50 Tips for Speaking Like a Pro.* Boston, MA: Course Technology, 1999.

Paulson, Terry, Ph.D. *Making Humor Work.* Boston, MA: Thomson, 1989.

Smart, Doug, et al. *303 Solutions for Boosting Creativity and Solving Challenges.* Roswell, GA: J&B Publishers, 2005.

Smart, Doug, et al. *303 Solutions for Communicating Effectively and Getting Results.* Roswell, GA: J&B Publishers, 2005.

Smart, Doug, et al. *303 Solutions for Reaching Goals and Living Your Dreams.* Roswell, GA: J&B Publishers, 2005.

Walters, Lilly. *What to Say When You're Dying on the Platform: A Complete Resource for Speakers, Trainers, and Executives.* New York, NY: McGraw-Hill, 1995.

Additional References

American Management Association International. "Principles of Adult Learning Handout," Overland Park, KS, February 1997.

Lantzy, Walt. "The Fundamentals of the Close." *American Management Association International Trainer Orientation Manual.* Overland Park, KS, July 1997.

Stanley, Mandi. *Hot Tips, Tools and Techniques for Making the Most of Every Early Childhood Professional Development Opportunity Leader's Guide.* Jonesboro, AR: Arkansas State University Childhood Services, 2004.

Stanley, Mandi. *How To Shine in Impossible Situations: A Crash Course in Dealing with Difficult Participants and Conditions.* Jonesboro, AR: Arkansas State University Childhood Services, 2004.

Stanley, Mandi. *My Success Recorder: An Interactive Guide for Capturing Creative Ideas That Work: A Trainer Orientation Gift.* Jonesboro, AR: Arkansas State University Childhood Services, 2004.

Special Thanks To

My veteran training managers between 1997 and 2002 at the American Management Association International's Padgett-Thompson and Keye Productivity Center one-day seminar divisions: Kay McClure, Michele Markey, Steve Dew, Walt Lantzy, Brian Healy, Noe Tabares, Cindy Swall, and Cynthia Sherwood

Aimee Onoszko, my client coordinator at The SpeakersTrust

My high school Speech I and Speech II teacher, Peggy Holmes, aka *pholmes*

The team at Pecan Row Press

Some Really Generous Speakers with Solid Messages and Great Platform Skills

Mark Sanborn, CSP, CPAE Speaker Hall of Fame

President
Sanborn & Associates, Inc., an idea studio for leadership development
Past president of the National Speakers Association
www.MarkSanborn.com
303-683-0714

Leadershipgurus.net lists Mark as one of the top 15 leadership experts in the world today. He is author of the international best-selling book *The Fred Factor* and has presented more than 2200 speeches and seminars in every state and 10 countries. In 2007 Mark was awarded The Ambassador of Free Enterprise Award by Sales & Marketing Executives International, and he is winner of the The Cavett through the National Speakers Association.

Naomi Rhode, CSP, CPAE Speaker Hall of Fame

Cofounder, SmartHealth
Past president of the National Speakers Association
Past president of the Global Speakers Federation
1997 Cavett Award winner
2003 Legend of the Speaking Profession recipient
NaomiRhodeCPAE@gmail.com

In addition to being a much-sought-after professional speaker and emcee, Naomi is the author of two inspirational gift books: *The Gift of Family - A Legacy of Love* and *More Beautiful Than Diamonds - The Gift of Friendship*, and has co-authored *Speaking Secrets of the Masters, Meditations for the Road Warrior* and many other multi-authored books.

Marilyn Sherman

Owner
UpFront Presentations
www.MarilynSherman.com
702-631-5700

Marilyn Sherman inspires audiences to get out of their comfort zone and live life in the front row.
Popular programs:
"Who Moved My Comfort Zone?"
"Why Settle for the Balcony? How To Get a Front-Row Seat in Life"

Terry Paulson, PhD, CSP, CPAE Speaker Hall of Fame

www.TerryPaulson.com
818-991-5110
Author of **The Optimism Advantage**

Popular programs:
"Leverage Your Optimism Advantage"
"Leaders Make Change Work"

Kimberly Medlock, CPO

Certified Professional Organizer
Productive Matters
Author of **Saving Time Matters**
www.KimberlyMedlock.com
662-893-7933

Program titles:
"Get More Time Out of Your Day"
"Get Organized Using Microsoft Outlook®"
"Getting it Done & Getting Along"
"Reducing Your Mental Clutter"

Joe M. Turner

Corporate Magic Communicator
Turner Magic Entertainment
www.TurnerMagic.com
404-644-6791

Specialties:
"Mind Magic: Tools and Techniques for Instantly Improving Your Memory"
"Doing the (Seemingly) Impossible in Your Organization"

Bobbe White

Speaker, Author, Certified Laughter Leader (seriously!)
Try Laughter! Inc.
www.TryLaughter.com
217-242-3705

Popular programs:
"Try Laughter—Just for the Health of It!"
"My Life's Out of Balance—and It's Worse Than my Checkbook!"
"Taking the Cuss out of Customer Service"

Amanda Box

Owner
Amanda Box Communication
www.AmandaBox.net
601-896-4622

Specialty topics: "Diversity Training," "Communication Through Change"

Pamela Jett, CSP

Owner
Jett Communication, Inc.
www.JettCT.com
803-831-2231

"Words Matter: Remarkable Communication Skills for Remarkable Results"

Janice Hurley-Trailor

The Image Expert
www.JaniceHurleyTrailor.com
480-219-2210

Keynote topics:

"How to Look Like a Million—Without Spending It"
"Business Etiquette"

Larry Mersereau, CTC

Owner
PromoPower
www.PromoPower.com
515-987-6071
Specialties:
"Branding, Positioning—Differentiation"
"Sales Motivation and Techniques"
"Marketing Strategies and Tactics"

Bert Decker

Decker Communications, Inc.
www.Decker.com
415-543-8100
Author of **You've Got to be Believed to be Heard**

Phil Hardwick

Stennis Institute of Government at Mississippi State University
Author of **The Great American Mystery Series**
www.PhilHardwick.com
601-594-3371
Retreat facilitator for chambers of commerce, economic development organizations,
and nonprofit organizations

Mark LeBlanc

Owner
Small Business Success
www.SmallBusinessSuccess.com
612-339-4890
Author of **Growing Your Business** and **Never Be the Same**
Flagship presentation: "Growing Your Business!"

Sid Salter

Host: "On Deadline With Sid Salter"
SuperTalk Mississippi (TeleSouth Communications)
Perspective editor/columnist: **The Clarion-Ledger**

✅ A Checklist of No-Panic Checklists!

Meet Your Author

HER CAREER in public speaking began years ago on a stage in front of 700 college freshmen. Talk about a tough audience!

Today Certified Speaking Professional Mandi Stanley has moved from the campus podium to the corporate classroom. She has traveled throughout North America entertaining and educating more than 40,000 seminar participants, totaling 4,000 platform hours. She works primarily with business leaders who want to boost their professional image and with people from all walks of life who want to be better speakers and writers. Some of her repeat clients include:

- McDonald's USA
- Campbell's Soup
- The United States Air Force
- Duke Energy Corporation
- Kimberly-Clark's World Headquarters
- Mississippi Bankers Association
- Southern Farm Bureau Life Insurance
- EastGroup Properties
- Fleet Readiness Center Southeast
- The Rockefeller University

Mandi is a professional member of the National Speakers Association, the leading organization for experts who speak professionally.

In 2003, she was designated a CSP, Certified Speaking Professional. Fewer than 9 percent of all worldwide speakers have earned this designation, and Mandi is the first Mississippian in history to receive this honor through the NSA.

She's a *summa cum laude* graduate from Mississippi State University, and in 1998 she received the quality award and Highest Market Share recognition for the American Management Association International's one-day seminar division. Audiences appreciate her platform enthusiasm, interactive style, and content-rich messages. Programs in her **No-Panic** seminar series include:

The No-Panic Plan for Presenters
No-Panic Proofreading
A No-Panic Approach to Business and E-Writing
*No-Panic Technical Writing for Engineers and Other Knowledge
    Workers*

She and her husband Bob enjoy living in Madison with their two young sons—but don't count on her writing ***The No-Panic Plan for Rearing Boys*** anytime soon!